THE MAGIC OF
WRITING

Write to Heal, Transform, & Transcend

SIRSHREE

The Magic of Writing
Write to Heal, Transform, and Transcend

By **Sirshree** Tejparkhi

Copyright © Tejgyan Global Foundation
All Rights Reserved 2024

Tejgyan Global Foundation is a charitable organization
with its headquarters in Pune, India.

ISBN : 978-93-90132-37-9

Published by WOW Publishings Pvt. Ltd., India

First edition published in November 2024

Printed and bound by Trinity Academy For Corporate Training Ltd, Pune

This book is based on the Hindi book titled,
Likhaan Niyam by **Sirshree** Tejparkhi

Copyright and publishing rights are vested exclusively with WOW Publishings Pvt. Ltd. This book is sold subject to the condition that it shall not by way of trade or otherwise, be lent, resold, hired out, or otherwise circulated without the publisher's prior written consent in any form of binding or cover other than that in which it is published and without a similar condition including this condition being imposed on the subsequent purchaser and without limiting the rights under copyright reserved above, no part of this publication may be reproduced, stored in or introduced into a retrieval system, or transmitted, in any form, or by any means, electronic, mechanical, photocopying, recording or otherwise, without the prior written permission of both the copyright owner and the above-mentioned publisher of this book. Any person who does any unauthorized act in relation to this publication may be liable to criminal prosecution and civil claims for damages.

Although the author and publisher have made every effort to ensure accuracy of content in this book, they hereby disclaim any liability to any party for any loss, damage, or disruption caused by errors or omissions, resulting from negligence, accident, or any other cause. Readers are advised to take full responsibility to exercise discretion in understanding and applying the content of this book.

*To those
who wielded their pen like a sword
to achieve remarkable feats.
They won their inner battle to
gain mastery over their mind.*

Content

Preface	7
PART 1 - INTRODUCTION	**11**
1. The Pen as a Compass	13
2. Abiding in the Source	16
3. Why Write	21
4. Obstacles in the Practice of Writing	27
PART 2 - THE LAWS OF WRITING	**31**
5. The First Law of Writing	33
6. The Second Law of Writing	36
7. The Third Law of Writing	39
8. The Fourth Law of Writing	41
9. The Fifth Law of Writing	43
10. The Sixth Law of Writing	46
11. The Seventh Law of Writing	49
PART 3 - GUIDELINES FOR EFFECTIVE WRITING	**53**
12. Start Small, But Be Consistent	55
13. Make Writing Interesting and Creative	57
14. Write to Organize	62
15. Write to Plan	67
16. Write to Record and Remember	75
17. Write to Ideate and Introspect	79
18. Write to Communicate	84
19. Write in the Air	90
20. The 21-day Challenge of Daily Writing	93

PART 4 - THERAPEUTIC WRITING — 95

21. Write to Heal — 97
22. Heal False or Limiting Beliefs — 102
23. Attain Freedom from the Past — 106
24. The Healing Power of Storytelling — 108

PART 5 - TRANSFORMATIVE WRITING — 113

25. Write to Reprogram Yourself — 115
26. Goal Setting and Visualization — 124
27. Scripting the Blueprint of Your Life — 129
28. Gratitude and Admiration — 138

PART 6 - TRANSCENDENTAL WRITING — 147

29. Connecting with the Source — 149
30. Writing from the Source — 159

Appendix — 169

Preface

Your Pen Holds the Ink for Your Future

The world is a divine fabric of existence woven by God with the threads of certain laws.

Once, at a job interview, candidates were asked, "What is the goal of your life? Where do you see yourself in the next five years?"

One of the candidates answered, "I want to become a sales manager." Another replied, "I want a lucrative job that will allow me to buy a mansion." A third candidate said, "I want to earn and fund my further studies abroad."

One candidate, however, opened his diary and showed his written goal. He had detailed the steps he would take to achieve the goal, even noted it on his smartphone, and set a reminder with its pictorial representation as his screensaver.

The interviewer was struck by the stark contrast between those who just superficially talked about their goals and the one who had precisely written down his goal.

Put yourself in the interviewer's shoes. Whom would you hire? Obviously, the one who had clearly and elaborately written down his goal.

Writing, indeed, makes all the difference, but you won't appreciate it unless you start writing. Initially, you might feel unsure about what to write and what difference it would make. You might regard it as a waste of time, but it isn't. Start writing about minor things; eventually, you will write even about the significant things. But be consistent and write at the right time.

The written word dispels the darkness of ignorance.

And the eye of wisdom opens to the dawn of a new life.

So, hesitate not! Understand the astounding power of writing and write your way to success because your pen holds the ink for your future. Start maintaining a journal, either on paper or digital, and write about the spiritual, mental, physical, financial, and social aspects of your life. This will help you understand yourself better, determine your life purpose, and shape your future.

Once you start reaping the benefits of consistent writing, your journal will become your closest companion, guide, and confidante. It will help you become a better version of yourself and transform your life into a book worth reading!

Your life is indeed a beautiful book; you are its author, editor, and central character. Unlike any movie, where the story is written for mere entertainment, you must write your life story to learn, evolve, and shape it. Every scene of your life is special to you because you are emotionally connected to it and eager to make it worthwhile.

In this book, you will find the most effective ways to script your life story. You will discover the highest potential of writing to catapult your life to its zenith.

To achieve this systematically, this book has been crafted into the following parts that guide you step-by-step.

1. Introduction

This part unveils the ultimate potential of writing, inspired by the very source of life. It discusses the shift from a mundane life to a life liberated by the realization of your true self—the Source, the Self, God, or Consciousness.

2. The Laws of Writing

In this part, you will understand laws that govern writing and how to leverage them for positive change.

3. Guidelines for Writing

In this part, you will discover practical guidelines and techniques to hone and sharpen your journalling practice.

4. Therapeutic Writing

In this part, you will learn how to use writing as a therapeutic tool to overcome past traumas, negative tendencies, and eliminate limiting beliefs to experience inner peace, clarity, and happiness.

5. Transformative Writing

This part guides you in effectively using writing to understand yourself better and direct your feelings and thoughts to create your desired future, leading to growth and lasting success.

6. Transcendental Writing

It is the will of the Source that everyone should live in love, joy, and peace and lead a fulfilling life. When you bestow blessings on yourself and others and offer positive words as a prayer for everyone, you lend your voice to the will of the Source.

Transcendental writing allows thoughts to emerge from the Source and flow naturally without reasoning or judgment. When you write down the will of the Source after understanding the laws of writing, your writing bears fruit.

Reading this book from start to finish will be more impactful than skipping ahead to specific sections or chapters. However, if a particular topic piques your interest, feel free to explore that section before resuming the sequential flow of chapters.

 Most chapters offer writing exercises and experiments, each marked with the symbol shown here for easy identification. Keep a journal handy, and use it frequently to engage with these exercises. The more thoughtfully and thoroughly you complete

each one, the deeper you can understand them and the more practical benefits you will gain from these concepts.

As part of Sirshree's comprehensive System for Wisdom, a growing body of knowledge guides all aspects of life—from practical living to spiritual growth. Where relevant, references to other related books are provided throughout this book. At the end of those chapters, you'll find QR codes to scan to book copies of these precious books of wisdom.

So, let go of hesitation and commence this journey. Pick up your pen and start writing.

PART 1

INTRODUCTION

1

The Pen as a Compass

Writing is not just a profession; it is a way of life

A police officer's son was kidnapped in his infancy and raised among a band of dacoits. He grew up believing he was one of them. His childhood was a turbulent journey through the lawless world of crime, where deceit and violence were the norm.

Driven by a notorious ambition, he sought to surpass a legendary dacoit's infamous record of killing fifty policemen. It was his means of asserting himself as a ruthless and feared figure in the underworld.

A day of horror shattered his world as he witnessed the gruesome killings in a village, including the innocent sacrifice of a little boy. The trauma of the child's suffering stirred dormant memories of his own past, igniting a flicker of doubt about his notorious ambition.

He began to question the authenticity of his ambition, wondering if it was truly his own or a product of the life he had been forced to live. As he delved deeper into his origins, a profound realization dawned upon him: he was not a dacoit; he was the son of an honest police officer.

This revelation caused a shift in his consciousness. The notorious ambition that had fueled his criminal life vanished. He realized his true nature was not rooted in destruction but in redemption. He yearned to break free from the cycle of violence and vowed to be a catalyst for change, leading the dacoits toward a path of reformation.

Like the dacoit, we often unknowingly adopt desires that are not our own; they stem from a distorted perception of who we are, a false identity we have clung to.

Realizing our true nature dissolves these inauthentic desires and reveals the auspicious will of our true self, the fulfillment of which alone gives lasting contentment.

Assessing what we truly need

You may question, "Is it wrong to have worldly desires? What's the harm in aspiring for fame or wealth?"

There is nothing inherently wrong with money or any other object of pursuit. However, the habit of pursuing something, assuming it will give lasting contentment, is inherently flawed. Honestly assess your real need.

Contemplate: Do these desires arise from peer pressure by observing what others value, or do they emerge from a clear understanding of who you truly are?

If you mistake a rope in the dark for a snake, you might search for a stick to beat the "snake." But do you really need the stick? What you really need is a torch that can help you see the rope as a rope. Then, the need for the stick will vanish, just as the dacoit's notorious desire vanished.

Once you use the torch of wisdom to realize who you truly are, all baseless desires will drop off, revealing your true need and leading to lasting fulfillment.

Writing as a compass to gain clarity and express the true self

In the modern world, where the pursuit of happiness has led to the need for instant gratification, the Law of Attraction and creative visualization have emerged as popular tools. These techniques, which posit that positive thoughts can manifest positive outcomes, have attracted a significant following. However, while these manifestation tools work, they are not a panacea.

To achieve lasting contentment, earnestly enquire, "What do I truly want?" It is here that the written word becomes a powerful ally. Writing is not merely a means of expression. It is a process of introspection, exploration, and discovery. By putting your thoughts on paper, you examine your desires, assumptions, beliefs, and fears with a detached perspective, identifying patterns and inconsistencies. Through this writing process, you gain clarity and uncover your essential nature.

When you clearly understand your essential nature, your desires become more aligned with your true self. Instead of being swayed by fleeting trends or societal expectations, you work toward meaningful, fulfilling, and authentic goals. This clarity of purpose provides a strong foundation for your decisions and actions.

Consider a writer who dreams of publishing a novel. If they approach this goal solely through the lens of the Law of Attraction, they may visualize themselves as a bestselling author without considering the necessary steps to achieve this. However, they should first write about why they want to write; what is waiting to be expressed from the source within them? By writing from inner inspiration rather than external aspirations, they can posit a higher purpose to their writing.

Moreover, writing can help you identify and address the underlying limiting beliefs that prevent you from achieving your goals. These beliefs, often formed in childhood or through past experiences, can unconsciously sabotage your efforts. By writing about your beliefs, you can bring them to the surface and examine them critically. You may discover that certain beliefs no longer serve you and can be replaced with more empowering ones.

In addition to providing clarity and direction, writing can be a source of solace and inspiration. When you feel overwhelmed or lost, writing can help you process your emotions and find meaning in your experiences. It can also connect you to the source of wisdom and creativity within you, giving you the strength and resilience to overcome challenges.

However, it is essential to note that writing is not a magic bullet. It requires discipline, patience, and a willingness to be honest with yourself. This book serves as a writing coach to guide you in your journey of transformation and transcendence.

2

Abiding in the Source

Writing is a creative journey, where every word creates a new world.

Imagine an artist who painted a picture of a paintbrush. And this paintbrush came alive and created more paintings for the artist! But one day, it suddenly forgot its original purpose and began to assume an individual existence and a separate purpose. It started painting by itself without consulting the artist.

Though the paintbrush was created to explore and manifest the artist's creative inspiration, it remained disconnected from the source that gave it life. Thereafter, it could only replicate what already existed on the canvas, making copies of what other paintbrushes had already made.

Similarly, as a paintbrush for the Creator, we often stray from the divine plan, pursuing our own individual strokes. While human creativity flourishes, true contentment remains elusive, for it is only in aligning with the divine purpose that we find lasting fulfillment.

The source of life is beyond thoughts

You are not just a thinking machine. Instead, the thinking machine is an instrument you use. Careful observation will show that you are not your body since you can observe your body and its sensations. Whatever is being observed is not the observer. Even your thoughts can be observed.

Take time to observe your thoughts as they arise and subside. As you practice this, you will find that you are not your thoughts. You are the knower of your thoughts, the knower of your mind. This knowing continues to exist even in the gap between thoughts.

This deep knowing or consciousness is the essence of life. It is the source of life. Everything arises from the Source. It is who you truly are, beyond your body and mind.

The Source[1] can be experienced as the sense of being alive and awake to whatever is happening. This song of aliveness is being played constantly; you are that song. Being aware of this song gives the experience of pure bliss, independent of the world, untouched by situations.

The Source is the wellspring of all creation and inspiration. When you do not tap into this, your thoughts tend to be limited by what you see in the world. You are shut off to novelty. You need to inculcate the practice of dipping into the inner stillness of the Source frequently. This enables you to bring blissful stillness into your thoughts, speech, and actions, imbued with freshness and creativity.

Inspired writing happens automatically when you connect with this inherent blissful state of the Source. When the inspiration of the Source guides your thoughts, life thrives, spreads novelty, engages in service to humanity, and achieves true success.

Three types of success

When people are asked about the definition of success, their answers fall into three categories: success from others' perspective, success from one's own perspective, and success from the standpoint of the divine plan. Understanding these three types of success[2] can help you determine what truly matters in your pursuit of fulfillment.

1. Success from others' perspective

The first type of success is how others perceive it. Today, society equates success with material achievements such as owning a large home, amassing wealth, holding a prestigious job, or enjoying fame and power. People often enforce the belief that if you have wealth, authority, or exceptional skills, you are accomplished. This materialistic notion of success suggests that only those who achieve these outward pursuits are successful. But is this truly the case?

Materialistic success does not necessarily guarantee happiness and contentment. Like the paintbrush disconnected from the artist's creative spark, those who pursue this type of success merely replicate what others have achieved on the world stage. Many who have attained material success will attest that such success alone does not guarantee a sense of completeness.

2. Success from our own perspective

The second type of success comes from our own perspective. It is our own sense of achievement based on what we set out to do. It is the satisfaction of deciding on a goal and accomplishing it.

For example, if you decide to become a carpenter and succeed, you are successful in your own eyes, regardless of whether others regard it as success.

Society may not always align with your personal ambitions. Others may consider becoming doctors or engineers as being successful. However, you may feel successful and complete by becoming a carpenter. This self-defined success reflects personal fulfillment independent of others' judgments.

However, this type of success also arises from the notion of being a separate individual with a personal purpose, disconnected from the divine plan.

3. Success from the perspective of the divine plan

The third and most profound type of success is achieved by aligning with the divine plan. You become what God intends you to be. You realize your true essence and manifest its qualities, thus becoming what you were meant to be. When the paintbrush aligns with the Creator's inspiration, it becomes the instrument to express limitless potential.

Success, in its most profound sense, is about completeness. But completeness from which perspective? Material success might leave you feeling incomplete; personal success may satisfy your ambitions but leave a sense of void within. Living according to the divine plan alone offers true completeness. You manifest your divine plan when you abide by the Source of life within and lend words to the inspiration that arises from the Source.

For this, you need to shift from the noise of incessant thoughts in the head to the tranquility of the heart. The distance between the head and heart is short, but many take a lifetime to bridge it, and some never do.

Living in the head, dwelling on endless thoughts, leads to confusion and instability. Thoughts based on the false assumption of being a limited individual distance you from the Source. Transcend this mental framework of a personality and connect with the Source within.

Negative thoughts cause entanglement as they manifest more negative experiences in life. To transcend the mind, first move from a negative mindset to a positive one before you can shift to a state beyond thoughts, both positive and negative.

Part 4 of this book, "Therapeutic Writing," explains practical writing techniques for eliminating negative impressions. Part 5, "Transformative Writing," helps you anchor positive feelings and thoughts, laying the ground for transcendence. Various writing methods have been provided that help lay the seeds for growth and success.

A positive mind is more conducive to transcendence. It facilitates going beyond and connecting with the Source within. Part 6, "Transcendental Writing," delves into the nuances and techniques for going beyond the mind and allowing writing to flow from the Source.

 [1] - To know more, read the book
The Source... Power of Happy Thoughts
by Sirshree.
Scan this QR code to order your copy.

 [2] - To know more, read the book
The Ultimate Purpose of Success
by Sirshree.
Scan this QR code to order your copy.

3

Why Write

It is a fact that writing is one of the few professions where you can excel without having had specialized education.
~ J.K. Rowling

In 1809, a boy named Louis was born in a small French village. Curious and playful, he was always exploring. At three, he injured his eye while playing, resulting in partial loss of vision. Shortly after, an infection blinded his other eye. Despite the darkness, Louis never lost hope. His parents nurtured his independence and encouraged him constantly. As a teenager, they sent him to the Royal Institute for Blind Youth in Paris to continue his education.

One day, Charles Barbier, a French army captain, visited the school. He had invented a tactile writing system called "night writing," enabling soldiers to communicate silently and without light on the battlefield. This system used raised dots and dashes to represent sounds. When he demonstrated it at the school, Louis was enthralled. Inspired by this system, he set out to create a more efficient, simplified, and accessible system.

Through imagination and hard work, Louis developed a script using raised dots to represent letters, numbers, and symbols. This script enabled the visually impaired to read and write, becoming known as Braille, named after Louis Braille. Today, even without sight, people can read and write using Braille, allowing them to communicate their thoughts and connect with others.

This example illustrates the importance of writing. Essentially, writing brings thoughts and ideas to life, acting as the written form of thinking.

Writing plays a crucial role in every field. In education, it helps students develop and articulate their thoughts clearly. In business, it ensures effective communication, presentation, planning, and reporting. In literature, it fosters cultural and social evolution, allowing clear expression of ideas in society. Writing is also vital to social structures like constitutions, laws, economics, and education systems. Besides these, other fields like science, arts, trade, and commerce are incomplete without written communication.

Throughout history, many great figures have written down their emotions, thoughts, and experiences for the benefit of others. For example, Rabindranath Tagore, a renowned poet and philosopher, left behind letters, poems, and essays. His writings, which address spiritualism as well as social issues and values, continue to inspire people even today.

Swami Vivekananda is recognized as a spiritual ambassador and visionary. He left a great legacy of letters, poems, essays, and speeches. His writings shed light on self-realization, the powers of the mind, and life mastery. His invaluable wisdom, guiding seekers toward spiritual growth is accessible to every generation through published texts.

Thus, writing helps to convey our thoughts to every corner of the world. Therefore, develop your writing skill and hone it regularly.

The benefits of writing

Once, a teacher was teaching science to students. As she began the class, students took out their notebooks to write notes. She instructed them not to write down anything until they truly understood it. The students seized this as an excuse not to write. They felt relieved to postpone notetaking for now and consider it later.

The entire year passed in this manner, and the exams approached. Without any written material to study, the students found themselves unprepared. They were unsure how to answer the exam questions. Many of them did not even have textbooks. Panic set in, and they tried borrowing notes from others, only to discover that everyone else was in the same predicament. All of them desperately needed notes.

One student felt that if he had taken down notes during classes, it would have helped him, and studying would not have been so challenging. He understood the consequences of not writing and resolved, "Whether I understand something or not, I must write. I must diligently take down notes. I must read what I have written to grasp and understand it better later."

You would have likely experienced this firsthand. You went to a bank or government office for work, and they asked you to submit necessary documents. At that time, you listened carefully and memorized the list, thinking you would not need to note it down. However, when you returned the next day, you discovered that some required documents were still missing. Now, you can understand the consequences of not taking notes. Therefore, as far as possible, do not underestimate any task; write it down to ensure your work is efficiently completed on time.

You may take a few minutes to write, but you will not regret it later, thinking, "Oh! If only I had written it down, I could have saved my time and energy today." Therefore, cultivate the habit of writing to achieve the best results.

Writing is often overlooked as a valuable activity. People underestimate its importance. But do you know the insights and realizations it can offer? If you want to lead a holistic life, where your feelings, thoughts, speech, and actions are aligned, you must integrate the practice of writing into it. Writing is as important as your feelings, thoughts, speech, and actions. Speak what you intend to do, do what you think, think what you feel, and write what you want.

Suppose 100 people who have completed their education and are not professional writers were asked how many still write regularly. Perhaps only 10% would say they do, and even they may write only occasionally. Therefore, it is essential to understand the importance of writing, as writing has been a significant part of the lives of those who have climbed the ladder of success.

Warren Buffet, the famous investor and one of the world's wealthiest people, also practices writing to bring clarity to his thoughts. Apple founder Steve Jobs also used writing to organize and present his new ideas.

No matter what stage of life you are in today, writing can bring a new turn to your life. You may wonder, "Why should I start writing again after a certain age?" Then, ask yourself another question, "Do I wish to develop myself? Do I want to achieve success? Do I want lasting contentment?" If so, the initial question becomes irrelevant because writing brings growth, success, and lasting contentment.

Let us explore some benefits of the practice of writing.

1. Enhances memory and retention

When you write, both your motor and sensory faculties work in unison. While your hand is writing, your mind is engaged in thinking. Simultaneously, as your eyes see the words, an image of the words is formed in your mind, which helps with retention. This enhances your memory, allowing you to recall what you have written even after a long period.

2. Unleashes creativity

When you write, you are free to harness your creativity fully. It provides an opportunity to express the talents and qualities within you.

3. Helps set goals and track progress

The art of consistent writing helps you document your goals and work toward them. If you write your goals in detail, you can periodically review and update them as needed.

4. Cultivates discipline and time management

Writing can bring discipline into your life. By using writing tools, you can effectively manage your time. The habit of keeping your tasks in writing not only conserves your energy but also saves your time.

5. Enhances self-introspection

Writing fosters personal growth. It brings clarity to your thoughts, motivating you to advance in life. It also cultivates the art of introspection as you review your past experiences while writing. It helps you revisit your mistakes and learn from them, building a strong resolve to avoid repeating them in the future. Consequently, many of your problems get resolved on their own.

Writing also allows you to understand your emotions, thoughts, and methods of working. It serves as feedback for yourself. When you write down your thoughts and revisit them later, it becomes easier to discern between right and wrong thoughts and constructive and unproductive ideas.

6. Emergence of new qualities

When you become free from anxiety, the enthusiasm to try something new arises within you and your latent qualities begin to emerge. Consistent writing helps bring out the hidden creative traits from within you. These traits can manifest as poetry, stories, essays, verses, or songs. When you engage in written introspection for self-improvement, you begin to understand yourself better, thereby enhancing the quality of your thoughts.

7. Writing as a self-therapy

For those who are trapped in depression, stress, or anxiety, regular writing can be an effective form of self-therapy. Some people hesitate to share their thoughts with others or may not be able to open up fully. Others may fear that sharing their issues could lead to gossip or worsen the situation. Writing is a blessing for such people. The habit of writing helps them break free from the web of stress, depression, and anxiety.

Whenever people pen their feelings, thoughts, and events in a diary, they find themselves feeling lighter within. Their negative emotions begin to dissipate, and they become physically and mentally healthier. Once they achieve complete well-being, they start viewing their life events from a new perspective and begin to enjoy life.

8. Generation of feel-good hormones enabling creativity

Psychologists state that when the subconscious mind's suppressed thoughts are written down, the brain releases a hormone called endorphin, which makes the writer feel good. This is often referred to as the "feel-good" hormone. When you write, you feel at ease with your emotions, which helps you feel better and regain a sense of control. This stimulates the parts of the brain responsible for enhancing creativity. Therefore, people who write regularly tend to feel better and are often more creative than others. Writing increases mental and cognitive ability, making the generation of new ideas more possible.

Despite so many benefits of the practice of writing, why do we still refrain from integrating this practice of writing into our lives? In the next chapter, we will understand the obstacles that dissuade us from using the magical power of writing.

4

Obstacles in the Practice of Writing

*Learning the art of discerning what to discard over time
and what to continue consistently is essentially
the highest preparation for written contemplation.*

Despite her desire to continue her education, Seema could not do so due to circumstances and got married at a young age. The following 17 to 18 years were spent fulfilling parental responsibilities. When her children got older and busy with their own lives, Seema had plenty of free time. This led to the resurfacing of her long-held desire to learn new languages. In today's digital age, mobile apps have made learning languages accessible to everyone. She decided to learn German and embark on a new endeavor. However, she faced challenges writing down important points to be remembered due to a lack of habit. The task seemed daunting, and she often thought, "Oh no! I have to write; I am not used to it, and I have always found it boring."

Nevertheless, she gradually began writing, though her speed was slow due to lack of practice. She missed many details, making it difficult to understand upon re-reading. Despite this, she continued to write and eventually learned German. Later, she shared her notes with other students learning German, thus helping them. In this way, she turned her obstacle into a powerful tool.

In today's fast-paced life, even educated people avoid writing, which has slowed down their personal development. A survey has shown that most people feel uncomfortable with writing and do not want others to read what they have written. Additionally, they face several obstacles in writing, such as:

1. "What is the use of writing?"

Many people question, "What is the use of writing?" They cannot appreciate the value of writing. Additionally, they often fear that their personal information might be disclosed, someone might read their diary, or it might fall into the wrong hands. Therefore, they prefer not to pen their thoughts.

2. Lack of writing habit

Nowadays, ready-made templates, formats, and Artificial Intelligence tools make constructing short messages and emails easy. As a result, people find it challenging to write in their own words. Due to a lack of practice, their handwriting is often untidy, and their vocabulary is weak, which hinders their writing.

3. Lack of a significant topic to start writing

Some people believe they should only start writing when they have a strong, interesting topic, so they never begin. Some feel it is essential to have a clear idea for writing and keep waiting for the right idea to emerge. Some avoid writing because they think it is a task meant only for professional writers.

4. Laziness

Some people know that writing is important, and they want to write. They even sit down with pen and paper, but due to laziness, they get caught up surfing the internet or talking to someone, thinking they will write later. However, you may have experienced what happens thereafter. What gets missed out often never gets documented later. Therefore, if you write down what you have learned immediately, you will appreciate yourself for this practice after a few days. Every successful individual or organization has progressed due to the habit of writing.

5. Waiting for the right mood

Some people wait for inspiration to strike before they start writing, hoping for a clear signal from within before they begin. However, they must understand that waiting for the right mood is unnecessary. Instead, they should pick up a pen and start writing a few lines on paper. Even if they end up tearing it later, developing the habit of writing is what truly matters.

6. No time to write

This is the most prominent excuse people often quote. Due to a lack of time management skills, their time gets consumed by trivial or unnecessary tasks, and by evening, they feel they have too much work and no time left for writing.

7. Reluctance to revisit old wounds and memories

Many people avoid writing about their past experiences because it can stir up old emotions and cause them distress. They fear that revisiting these memories might trigger anxiety or depression, and they are reluctant to open up or share their feelings with others.

8. Where and how to write?

Many people are confused about where and how to write—whether to buy a notebook, use a diary, or write on a laptop or tablet. Since they do not have an effective way of writing, this question remains unresolved, and they never begin writing.

While these obstacles may seem significant, once you begin writing, you can truly appreciate its importance. Writing can help fulfill many of your repressed desires, heal old wounds, reach new heights of personal development, and execute plans with newfound confidence.

PART 2

THE LAWS OF WRITING

5

The First Law of Writing

Our karma, or deeds, typically include our speech and actions that are visible in the world. However, our thoughts and feelings, though invisible to the world, are subtler forms of karma that yield results and impact our lives behind the scenes.

In the same way, written words also work in the unseen. Writing down our feelings and thoughts energizes our actions and speeds up the manifestation of results. Hence, expressing our thoughts and feelings through mindful writing is a higher form of karma.

First Law

Writing bridges the visible and invisible forms of karma, speeding up the manifestation of its outcome and the resulting feelings.

Although written words are visible, our thoughts, feelings, and experiences reside unseen in the mind. Writing is the medium that expresses them, bridging the seen and unseen worlds.

Every word has its own vibration. When you consciously speak positive words, their vibrations spread everywhere, gradually improving your life. However, when written, these vibrations spread faster and wider. This occurs in the unseen, so you may not immediately notice the results that written karma brings you.

 Exercise

Let us perform an experiment to understand this law.

In the Hindu tradition, it is common to chant the name of God 108 times. People also repeat affirmations. This experiment is similar. Pick any positive word, such as love, joy, peace, courage, silence, faith, or any name of God, like Rama, Shiva, Christ, or Allah.

In the first part of this experiment, keep this book aside and set an alarm for one minute. Close your eyes and silently repeat your chosen word in your mind until the alarm goes off. After one minute of continuous repetition, note what you experienced.

For the second part of this experiment, take the same word and write it repeatedly in your notebook for one minute. Note what you experienced.

You will gain an important insight from this experiment. Chanting is an activity that engages the mind. However, we all know how restless our mind is, making it difficult to stay focused. It constantly jumps from one thought to another, just like a monkey.

On the other hand, when you write a positive word or name, your entire focus shifts to the act of writing. As you write, the word occupies your mind, allowing your hand, eyes, and thoughts to focus on one thing. You likely noticed being fully absorbed during the experiment. This demonstrates how writing aligns your feelings, thoughts, speech, and actions in the same direction.

True progress happens when these five pillars of karma—feelings, thoughts, speech, writing, and actions—are aligned. Your feelings, thoughts, speech, and actions are a spontaneous part of your life, requiring no conscious effort. However, writing is not a default activity and demands deliberate effort to start. With practice, writing can become as habitual as your feelings, thoughts, speech, and actions.

For many people, reading and writing are an essential part of life only when they are in school or university. After graduation, they believe their karma only relates to their occupation, business, or social relations. For them, karma is only an external action. They don't see thinking, feeling, or writing as effective forms of karma. This limited understanding deprives them of the potential benefits of writing.

If you view your life on Earth as a school where you are constantly learning, you will realize that, like students, writing and reading are an integral part of your karma. Just as students face exams, life tests you, too. When faced with life's trials, your karma, when imbued with writing, comes to fruition with a new force.

Although traditional writing on paper has declined with time, the habit of writing continues to grow digitally. New forms of language are emerging, from formal email communication to informal social media lingo. Everyone writes and posts on social media, often expressing negative words and ideas. However, many fail to recognize writing as a form of karma, remaining unaware of the negative vibrations they create and the consequences they will face.

To break this cycle of negative karma, focus on positive writing and send inspiring messages to others. This will not only benefit others but also improve your internal state and spread positive vibrations everywhere.

6

The Second Law of Writing

During India's struggle for independence, the idea of a free nation was initially just a dream. People felt bound by British rule, but some brave individuals dared to articulate this vision aloud. They spoke passionately about a future where no one would be enslaved, and their words began to resonate with the masses. As they communicated their message, the dream of freedom began to take shape, and more voices joined the cause.

These pioneers went door to door, explaining the significance of freedom and rallying support. Leaders organized gatherings to strategize, but initially, attendance was limited to local groups. Reaching people from other towns was challenging and dangerous. Yet, through persistent and courageous communication, the vision of a free India gained momentum. The spoken word became a powerful tool in uniting people and igniting a nationwide movement for independence.

Soon, activists began creating and distributing pamphlets with their ideas, reaching people in various towns. The written word proved more effective than speech alone. While spoken words were subject to interpretation, written words provided clarity and consistency.

Encouraged by the impact, some leaders launched their own newspapers. They published inspiring articles, poems, and anecdotes that fueled the passion for freedom. These written works complemented stirring speeches and mass gatherings, deepening the sense of patriotism.

As these messages took root in the hearts of many, they united more people in the struggle for independence. The written word, along with spoken inspiration, became a powerful force in the movement to free India.

The second law underscores the importance of the written word.

Second Law

More potent than thoughts is speech with clear intent.

More powerful than speech are words written mindfully.

Let us understand this in depth. The first part of this law states that speech holds more power than thoughts. You know how some words, when spoken, can pierce through like an arrow, causing deep hurt. When someone harbors thoughts of ill will for another, it troubles them internally. But when these thoughts are spoken aloud, they affect both the speaker and the listener.

In the same vein, good parents deliberately overlook their children's bad behavior, although they keep thinking about how to guide them toward progress. However, when the right opportunity arises, if they engage in clear discussions with their children, it leads to constructive solutions.

Thoughts keep boggling the mind. If you only ruminate on them internally, it is difficult to reach any conclusion. But when you open up and discuss these thoughts with someone, they gain direction, making it easier to arrive at a conclusion.

Now, let us consider the second part of this law, which states that the written word is more powerful than speech. Historically, written words have held more power than spoken words. Ancient kings and emperors used written messages or decrees sent via messengers to ensure the message was not distorted by the messenger's limited memory or lack of understanding of the message. Written decrees conveyed authority and were crafted with great thought and deliberation, ensuring every aspect of the message was precise and intentional.

You wouldn't give a wedding invitation too much importance unless you receive the actual invitation card. Similarly, when friends casually discuss meeting up, no one takes it seriously until someone writes a common message in the group, like, "Let's meet at that restaurant at this time." The impact is much greater, and the chances of everyone attending increase significantly. Writing down ideas gives them a solid anchor, helping them materialize faster into reality.

The written word has contributed more to human progress than any other mode. When thoughts are verbalized, they set actions in motion. Else thoughts remain as thoughts alone. However, when words are written on paper, they gain substantial influence. Remember: "More potent than thoughts is speech with clear intent. More powerful than speech are words written mindfully."

7

The Third Law of Writing

In a small town, there lived a man named Shekhar who spent his days lazing around, building castles in the air with his dreamy imagination. One day, he found a magic wand that could fulfill any desire. He wished for a grand palace, and instantly, a magnificent palace materialized before him. However, the palace was empty, so he asked for all the comforts and luxuries, and they appeared. Next, he wished for caretakers, housekeepers, and servants, and they all manifested immediately.

Now, Shekhar didn't know what tasks to assign them. He asked them to cook, but the palace had no groceries. He waved the magic wand and heaps of food appeared. Distressed by the abundance, he willed them to disappear. Gradually, the responsibilities of the servants, the palace, and luxuries overwhelmed him. He waved the wand again, making everything disappear. In an instant, it was all gone. Suddenly, Shekhar woke up and realized it was, thankfully, just a dream.

Thoughts like Shekhar's, which arise in a dream or without awareness, never come to fruition. They manifest only when they are empowered with awareness and passion. The second Law of Thought[1] is the Law of Direction, which states that when thoughts or desires are repeated with awareness and passion, they turn into reality. The Third Law of Writing is an extension to this Law of Thought.

---

[1] - Refer to *The Source* book to understand the Laws of Thoughts.

Third Law

Mindful writing empowers desires, significantly increasing the likelihood of their manifestation.

This means when a desire or thought is put into writing, its intensity increases, making it easier to turn into reality. Writing structures thoughts, giving them form because the right words are chosen. Additionally, every detail of how and when the desire should be fulfilled is documented. Reading these written desires later empowers them, increasing the likelihood of achieving them.

Writing down your thoughts and desires clarifies them, preventing confusion. It ensures clear communication with the Universe. When you write down your desires, you fix them, identifying and eliminating stray thoughts and needless desires in the process. You write only what you really want. Moreover, writing a desire or thought attaches feelings to your words, empowering the desires when they are re-read.

Every thought carries a feeling, and every word has its own vibration. Positive thoughts bring positive feelings, and positive words create positive vibrations.

Thus, when a positive thought is brought into writing with well-chosen words, the energy of those words attracts similar energies like love, happiness, enthusiasm, solace, and contentment. These energies collectively empower the desire, drawing it into your life. Positive words facilitate growth, while negative words create obstacles in their way.

Unsuccessful people tend to dwell on problems, while successful people always discuss solutions, opportunities, and possibilities. Therefore, write about solutions, opportunities, and possibilities, not problems. When you write what you truly want, it begins to manifest. Every thought influences your energy and shapes your experiences. This law applies to everything, big or small. You can shape your life as you wish by putting your desires into writing.

8

The Fourth Law of Writing

In a village, a young man once bought a large mirror and placed it outside his house. Whenever he stepped out, he would glance at his reflection. Over time, he noticed something peculiar—when he was happy, the mirror seemed to smile, and when he was sad, the mirror would cry. At first, he thought it was his imagination. But as it happened repeatedly, he started observing the mirror closely. He realized that the mirror smiled less and cried more often as he became more irritated over various issues. It didn't take time for him to understand that the mirror was reflecting the state of his mind.

It is a well-known proverb that the mirror never lies; it reflects us exactly as we are. Writing works similarly as a mirror on paper that reflects our emotions and thoughts through words. Whenever we write about what is going on within us, whether it is happiness, sorrow, anxiety, or any other problem, we transform these feelings into words and put them on paper. Writing is a mirror of the mind.

Fourth Law

> Writing serves as a mirror for the mind, revealing its truth.

Exercise

Let us understand this principle with an experiment. Write about an incident that occurred during the last two to three days in your diary. The incident could be positive, negative, or neutral. Now recall the incident: what was happening around you then, what were your emotions, how were you feeling, and so on. Write down a detailed description of the incident.

While writing, what did you feel? What were your emotions and thoughts? Did you honestly write everything as it had happened? If so, you would have noticed that what you wrote was your truth. Your writing served as a mirror for you. Through writing, you understood more about your state during that incident and your thoughts at that time. You relived that incident exactly as it was, seeing your reflection in the writing.

Your feelings often lie beneath the surface, like a hidden ocean. You might notice big waves of anger or sadness, but the deeper currents are usually hidden. Writing can help you unravel these hidden depths. It is like a map that reveals the intricate landscape of your emotions.

As you write, you peel off the layers of your feelings, revealing what is hidden and the things you really want. Each word is like a brushstroke, painting a picture of your deepest thoughts and feelings.

Writing helps you connect with your inner self without masks. You can explore your feelings more fully, understand why you feel in certain ways, and find comfort in knowing you are not alone.

In the quiet moments of writing, you can discover the hidden truths buried deep inside. You can face your fears, heal your wounds, and find a new purpose in life. Writing is more than just expressing yourself; it is a journey of self-discovery that helps you understand yourself and your place in the world.

9

The Fifth Law of Writing

Have you ever wondered where negative words or sentences come from: your head or your heart? And where do positive thoughts originate? Let us understand this through some experiments. First, read all the instructions, then practice the experiments one by one.

 Experiment 1

Recall any negative incident. Now, close your eyes and try saying negative sentences about that event. For example, if you have argued with someone in your neighborhood, try saying sentences like, "I am very angry with that person. If he weren't older than me, I would have given him a piece of my mind. What does he think of himself?!"

Now, choose three to four words related to that incident, such as anger, hatred, fear, sadness, worry, and so on. Write them down ten times in your journal. While doing this activity, focus on where these thoughts are coming from and where their impact is being felt. Is it the head or the heart?

 Experiment 2

Now, close your eyes and think of some positive sentences for the same incident, such as "Let it go! They are older than me. I love them. They take good care of me. What difference does it make if they say something?"

Repeat the same process with positive words such as love, joy, happiness, peace, acceptance, etc., and write them down ten times. Notice where these words come from: your head or your heart?

After this experiment, you will likely notice that negative thoughts and words arise from the head, while positive thoughts often come from the heart. If the experiment is performed correctly, you can clearly feel the difference.

When you write a positive thought about any incident repeatedly, your feelings associated with that incident begin to change.

 Writing changes your feelings, thoughts, and mood, giving them the right direction.

Fifth Law

Writing serves as a bridge between the head and the heart. When negative thoughts arise, acknowledge them and replace them with positive thoughts, writing them down repeatedly. This practice will not only change your feelings but also transform your perspective, helping you feel more connected to your heart. As a result, love will flow from your heart for everyone. The feelings of hatred, jealousy, or comparison will diminish. The negative thoughts that were bothering you will fade away.

At the same time, when you write your negative thoughts mindfully, you organize your thoughts and try to understand them clearly. When you repeatedly read what you have written, you gain new insights. When you write about your situation, experiences, and problems, solutions begin to emerge while writing. You begin to perceive your thoughts from a new perspective, leading to a shift in your thinking and a fresh approach to assessing your feelings.

In this way, writing not only channels your thoughts and feelings in a new direction but also helps transform them.

10

The Sixth Law of Writing

The proprietor of a cosmetics company conceived the idea of creating an organic kajal, free from harmful chemicals. He brainstormed several essential qualities: it should be gentle on the eyes when applied, should not cause allergies, resist smudging, not interfere with vision, etc.

However, during the initial phase, he had concerns about the product's effectiveness and market acceptance. To address this, he organized a meeting with the Product Design Team and presented the idea. The response was overwhelmingly positive, with everyone eager to develop and launch the product.

When the proprietor discussed the idea aloud with this team, it gained strength and built self-confidence in all of them. The team rallied around the initiative, enabling him to present the idea to the rest of the departments. A comprehensive project writeup was then created for the development and launch of the product. This document detailed every aspect, including tasks and responsibilities for each team involved. It outlined the desired qualities of the product, the ingredients, the sourcing and costing of raw materials, quality assurance measures, research, experimentation, and testing for the best mix of the ingredients. It also covered market research on the need for such a product, what would make it unique, feedback from testers on various versions, and the launch strategy. With every detail recorded, the complete framework for the product and its project was clear. Since everything was well documented, all the issues that emerged were easily addressed, leading to the smooth and successful launch of the product.

Just imagine what could have happened if the proprietor had never discussed this idea with his team. Or even if he had discussed the idea but never documented anything. Would the new product have ever seen its launch? Most likely, it would have remained just a fleeting thought. Without the power of detailed written planning, the idea would have lacked the necessary clarity and momentum, leaving it unrealized.

Writing creates space for ideas to emerge, developing into a coherent, evolving structure.

Sixth Law

Writing is like a fertile garden where ideas are planted and nurtured. Just as a tiny seed can grow into a towering tree, a simple thought can blossom into a large, intricate structure. When you put pen to paper or fingers to keyboard, you create a space where ideas can emerge, develop, and evolve.

As you write, your thoughts begin to take shape, like a sculptor molding clay. You can add, subtract, and rearrange them until they form a coherent and meaningful whole. Writing allows you to explore different perspectives, challenge your assumptions, and discover new connections between seemingly unrelated ideas. It is a process of discovery, a journey into the depths of your own mind.

The more you write, the more your ideas become interconnected and interdependent. They begin to form a web of relationships, where each thought is connected to countless others. This interconnectedness gives your writing depth and richness, making it more than just a collection of words. It becomes a living, breathing entity, capable of inspiring, informing, and even transforming you.

Writing also allows you to develop your critical thinking skills. As you analyze your ideas and the ideas of others, you learn to evaluate facts, identify fallacies, and develop perspectives based on sound reasoning.

This ability to think critically is essential to succeed in all areas of life, from education or profession to relationships.

In short, writing is a powerful tool for self-expression, creativity, and intellectual growth. It is a space where ideas can take root, grow, and flourish, creating a rich and complex tapestry of thought. By embracing the power of writing, you can unlock your full potential and make a lasting impact on the world.

11

The Seventh Law of Writing

Very often, when people face problems, thoughts associated with it can always keep troubling them. They get preoccupied with finding ways to solve their problems. But in a state of restlessness and distress, they are unable to pay heed to solutions they encounter. Seeing no forthcoming solutions, they get exhausted and give up, thinking, "Nothing is going to happen. Let me think over this later."

However, the moment they shift their focus away from the problem, the solution to their problem appears out of nowhere. How does this happen? This happens because when they let go and surrender everything to Nature, Nature works for them.

Similarly, when you start writing about your problems or worries, you eventually run out of thoughts as everything gets expressed on paper, leaving you feeling empty. When your mind becomes empty, you reach a state where no thoughts arise. This is a crucial state. In this thoughtless state, a new idea emerges from within. Later, you might believe that you got the idea after much thinking. But this happens only after the mind becomes empty and shifts its focus away from the problem. In this relaxed state of mind, you connect to the wise voice of the Source within you.

Seventh Law

Writing empties the mind, allowing the inner wise voice of the Source to express itself

When the mind is still and quiet, we can tap into a deeper level of consciousness, a wellspring of wisdom and creativity. The ideas that arise from this state are often original, intuitive, and novel. They are not the product of conscious thought but rather inspired by what lies beyond the mind.

To access this state of mind, we must learn to cultivate emptiness. This does not mean suppressing our thoughts or denying our emotions. Rather, it means shifting our focus away from the constant stream of mental activity and toward the background of consciousness. By doing so, we create the space for something new to emerge.

As we cultivate emptiness, we become more receptive to the subtle whispers of the Source. These whispers are not always loud or obvious, but they are always present. They are the quiet voice that speaks as our intuition, the spark of creativity, the guiding light that leads us toward peace, contentment, and creative expression.

When we connect with the Source within us, we receive answers far beyond our limited understanding. These answers are often surprising, inspiring, and profoundly transformative. By learning to empty the mind, we can tap into the wisdom of the Universe and unlock our full potential.

Part 6 of this book delves into the deeper aspects of connecting with and writing from the Source.

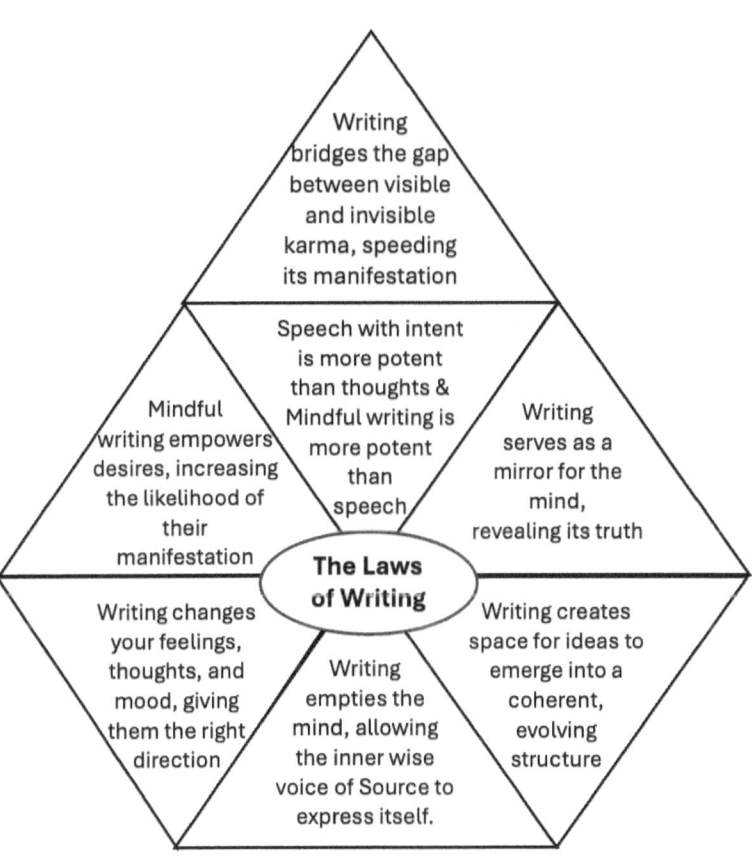

PART 3

GUIDELINES FOR EFFECTIVE WRITING

12

Start Small, But Be Consistent

The scariest moment is always just before you start.
~ Stephen King

Stephen King was born into a poor family. At 12, he started working to support his education and help his mother. He had a hobby of reading stories, which later led to a passion for writing. At one point, he sent one of his stories to the popular magazine Startling Mystery Stories.

For a long time, he received no response, which left him feeling disheartened. One morning, he received news that the editor had liked his story and that he would be paid for it. Although the payment was quite modest, Stephen was thrilled about his success. For the first time, he felt that writing could change his life. Despite financial constraints, he continued to write persistently. His dedication and consistency led him to become a renowned storyteller. Today, Stephen attributes his success to his regular writing.

This story illustrates that regular writing can change your life. Although it may seem that only writers can benefit from regular writing, it is not so. An ordinary person can also benefit in various aspects of life by consistently writing about their daily matters. For those seeking personal growth, satisfaction, and success, writing acts as a railing to support them as they move forward.

So, start writing. You might have many questions about when, what, and how to write, but despite these thoughts, make sure you write. Begin by writing before you go to bed at night; at the very least, jot down what you did throughout the day. If you are unable to write, record it on your smartphone instead.

For example, write down what you did after waking up: took shower, had breakfast, and chatted with your family before heading to work. Mention your mode of transport, whether you drove, took the bus, or rode your bike. Also, write down what you accomplished at the office, even if it is just 2 to 3 sentences.

Write down what you did after returning home in the evening, whether you watched TV, talked to your children, made phone calls, or anything else. After writing, go to bed. If you write this much on the first day, you will likely feel motivated to continue the next day. Writing will bring you peace and boost your courage to keep going. The initial unfamiliar hesitation will begin to fade. Even if you write similar things every day, consistency is the key. You will discover that you have plenty to write about in a few days.

Remember, maintaining consistency in writing is essential. With regular practice, skills that once seemed unattainable become achievable. Writing is a form of magic, and you will witness its transformative effects in your life.

 Exercise

Write down what you did today in the morning, afternoon, and evening.

13

Make Writing Interesting and Creative

*The hardest part of writing is putting
the right words in the right order on paper.*

A mother wanted to teach her daughter cooking, but the daughter kept procrastinating as she disliked cooking. She avoided entering the kitchen even though she knew that cooking was an essential skill for everyone. This became a challenge for the mother. Then the mother came up with a creative solution.

Seeing her daughter's love for cakes and ice cream, she found a dessert-making class in which the daughter eagerly enrolled. This eventually sparked her interest in cooking and led her to explore other recipes.

This same approach can be applied to writing or any other skill. Even if you appreciate its importance, if you do not make it interesting, there is a risk that you might lose interest and give up on it.

Think back to school when you enjoyed learning because of the diverse teaching and learning styles. Each teacher explored different aspects of a subject in their own creative ways. You might have developed a stronger interest in a subject due to a particular teacher's teaching style, even if you didn't like the subject before. Similarly, once you start writing and begin to enjoy it, the next step is to make it interesting and creative.

You might wonder why you should strive to make your writing interesting and creative when you are already engaged in writing. However, whether you like it or not, putting in the effort to make your writing creative and interesting is essential to fully benefit from the practice. This approach requires letting go of your old mindset and embracing consistent practice, an open mind, and a sense of playfulness. Doing so will inspire your imagination and make you feel contented.

Focus on language and words

Following are some guidelines on how language can make your writing creative and interesting.

1. Use minimum words

A family practiced writing a quotation daily, which helped everyone gain more knowledge in just a few words. Even their visitors benefited from it.

Similarly, you should clearly understand the topic you want to write about to express it concisely. For example, many writers have condensed vast texts into succinct aphorisms. Centuries-old couplets continue to inspire people to date. Couplets by Saint Kabir and Saint Rahim are still taught in schools. You must have often seen that some people send short messages daily that are eagerly awaited. These messages are concise and expressed in minimal words, making them easy to remember and enjoyable to read.

2. Simple language

When an artist learns to draw, they start with random lines, knowing they are in the learning process. Similarly, when you begin writing, even if your language is simple and your handwriting and choice of words are not yet refined, understand the purpose behind your writing. Initially, you are writing to develop the habit of writing; gradually, you can work on making it more engaging and polished.

Write in simple, clear language so that you can read it in one sitting. Use words that are easy to understand. Keep sentences short and straightforward. Even if you use colloquial language, ensure the words are simple. For example, words like "happy" or "fast" are simple, while words like "euphoric" or "expeditious" are complex.

3. Good handwriting

A doctor prescribed two medicines to a patient. Many pharmacies could recognize the name of one medicine but not the other from the prescription. Frustrated, the patient returned to the doctor for clarification. Even the doctor struggled to recognize his own handwriting!

Avoid writing in a way that makes it difficult to decipher. You are writing for yourself, not for someone else. Write in a manner that allows you to easily read and understand whenever you want. If you cannot understand your own handwriting, there is no point in writing.

Enhance writing with creativity

The modern mindset holds the notion that only the tangible is valuable. Due to a lack of awareness and discernment, people often prioritize superficial aesthetics over core values. Hence, they focus more on what is visually appealing, deeming it valuable regardless of its intrinsic worth.

Rekha and Nisha were tasked with delivering presentations. When presented, Nisha's presentation captivated the audience, while Rekha's presentation garnered only a fleeting glance. Despite covering all the essential points systematically, Rekha's presentation seemed rather dull. In contrast, Nisha made her presentation visually appealing and engaging. She used various colors, larger fonts for headings, underlined keywords, and highlighted key information. In essence, she used all possible means to make her presentation appealing and attention-grabbing. Thus, while content is crucial, it accounts for only 10%; a visually well-crafted presentation can draw people in and inspire them to explore the remaining 90%.

Keeping this in mind, strive to make your writing compelling. While your thoughts may be crucial, presenting them with impressive language in a well-crafted manner can make them more engaging and less likely to bore you upon rereading. When you adopt a creative approach, you allow yourself the opportunity to express your latent creativity and feelings. This not only inspires you to reread your own writings but also benefits others. Although you are doing this for yourself, incorporating creative elements in your writing can make it more effective. For example, when you give a gift to someone, while the content matters, the recipient's joy doubles when the gift is elegantly wrapped.

Let us understand different ways of enhancing your writing.

1. Use different colors and highlight text

When writing your thoughts or describing events, consider using different colors. For example, you may use blue or orange for a happy event to quickly identify it later. Reserve brown or grey for moments of trouble or confusion. Choose colors that suit your preferences. To emphasize key points or lessons learned, write them in uppercase or underline them for clarity during review.

2. Use symbols and pictures

Nowadays, a wide variety of symbols and emojis are available for use in various contexts. When writing a daily diary or reflecting on an important topic, you can add pictures to enhance clarity and understanding. For example, adding a smiley face to certain entries can help alleviate stress.

3. Use figurative language or idioms

Idioms are excellent for expressing your thoughts and emotions in fewer words. Sometimes, phrases used by others can be impactful. Hence, take note of appealing words and use them in your writing to enhance its richness. A strong command of language allows you to convey your feelings and thoughts more effectively. You can also add humor to your writing. Sometimes, profound insights written humorously can bring a smile to your face and convey the meaning more effectively.

Besides these, you can explore various other techniques to enhance your creativity.

Use mind maps

As you develop the habit of writing, you begin to consider various topics. However, despite having ample information on a subject, you may still struggle to express it. In such cases, a mind map serves as an excellent tool.

It harnesses creativity through the use of pictures, colors, and keywords, making it easier to organize your thoughts and write effectively about the topic.

Follow these steps to create a mind map.

- Choose a topic and identify its central theme. Write this theme in the center of the page.
- Surround it with related information using brief keywords or short phrases instead of long sentences. Use minimal words to keep your mind map concise and clear.
- Incorporate pictures, colors, and symbols wherever necessary.

You can creatively design a mind map in various forms. For example, a mind map with a tree-shaped outline can represent the central theme as a trunk, with its branches, leaves, flowers, and fruits symbolizing other details. Alternatively, you can experiment with different shapes like a hand, a musical instrument, or a clock to create your mind maps.

You will find mind maps summarizing the key points at the end of some chapters.

14

Write to Organize

*Inculcate the habit of writing to bring integrity
to your feelings, thoughts, speech, and actions.
This will help you overcome the habit of procrastination and forgetfulness.*

As soon as the phone rang, Arun answered it. He quickly jotted down an important number his uncle gave him on a newspaper. However, later, he couldn't recall where he had written it. He searched the entire house but couldn't find it. If he had written it in a contact diary, finding it would have been much easier.

Nowadays, it is not just diaries; everyone has smartphones to store numbers. However, if you don't save a number with the correct name, it can be hard to find it later. By organizing tasks systematically, you can save time that would otherwise be spent searching.

Similarly, in school, children have separate notebooks for each subject to keep their study material organized for exams. However, as they progress to college, they rely on fewer notebooks or even use a different one daily. When studying for exams, they struggle to find their notes or recall where they wrote them. If they organize their notes systematically, they can avoid this stress during exams.

If you develop the habit of planning and organizing tasks, you can complete them systematically with less stress. This is a valuable habit to nurture. When creating your diary or notebook, ensure to record everything in an organized manner. To keep it simple, you can divide it into 3 to 4 sections, as too many sections will require you to switch diaries often.

Here are some suggestions for sections you can create in your diary[3].

1. Wish list

Writing down your wishes will remind you to take steps toward fulfilling them whenever you see or read them.

2. Financial notes

Create a comprehensive list to track your significant current and future expenses. Outline your plans and how you intend to fund them. For example, if you plan to take a loan for a car or house, write down all the details in this section. Also, include plans for major future expenses like children's education, marriage, emergencies, retirement, healthcare, and insurance. This will help you stay financially organized.

3. Health notes

With lifestyle changes and work-related stress affecting nearly everyone, focusing on your physical and mental well-being is essential. In this section, list the steps you are taking to maintain your health now and in the future. Include activities that help you stay fit and note any changes you wish to make over time.

4. Daily learnings

Reflect on your daily experiences and learnings. Capture insights from new discoveries, interactions with others, or lessons from your own experiences. Even small events can help you learn valuable lessons and documenting them ensures they stay with you for the future.

5. Gratitude

Express your gratitude to those who support and assist you unconditionally on a daily basis. Write down your appreciation for their kindness and assistance. This will remind you of the blessings bestowed on you.

6. Common information

Keep a section for birth dates, anniversary dates, frequently used medicines, and important information, such as bank account numbers, encoded for security.

Besides this diary, always carry a small pocket diary and pen to jot down any memorable words or sentences you encounter, ensuring you don't forget them.

Organizing everything systematically benefits both you and those around you. In addition to using paper diaries, consider using a digital diary, which we will explore next.

 Exercise

List the sections you will include in your diary

Become tech-savvy

Become skilled and knowledgeable in using technology for tasks like writing and journaling. In today's world, devices from smartphones to laptops are essential for daily living. While the younger generation is often tech-savvy, the older generation is also adapting, which is crucial in today's digital world. No matter how old you are, don't think, "I've never used a computer before, so how can I learn?" With determination, anything is possible.

Many people were initially unfamiliar with computers but learned to use them when the need arose. Despite facing challenges and occasional lapses, consistent practice led them to proficiency. With wholehearted dedication, any skill can be mastered. If you have not yet learned to send messages from a mobile phone, use a computer to find and share information or send emails. It is essential to learn these skills quickly. This will enable you to access news, navigate to any destination virtually, and digitize tasks from the comfort of your device at home.

Embrace modern technology to streamline your work. Equip yourself with the right skills to achieve your goals. Although you won't learn these new abilities overnight, with time, as you practice them and start applying them, you will be amazed at the benefits.

Those who embrace new tools are better equipped to tackle future challenges. By dedicating a little time each day to learning from someone knowledgeable, you can streamline all tasks, from household chores to external responsibilities.

Today, nearly everyone owns a smartphone. Modern smartphones are equipped with essential tools like reminders, schedulers, calendars, list managers, worksheets, and word processors. These tools simplify task management and make it easy to record and track important activities. Numerous apps are available for journaling. You can download a suitable app and start journaling right away. Enjoy unlimited pages, secured storage, and password protection for added privacy.

You can store important documents and bank information securely on your device, keeping them private. You can also preserve your cherished memories on your device. Whether you carry a diary or a smartphone, it is always with you, allowing you to quickly jot down notes or capture photos of noteworthy moments. No matter how crucial the documents are, there is no risk of losing them, even if your phone is lost, because your data is securely saved in cloud storage. With so many benefits, it is compelling to start writing on your smartphone, laptop, tablet, or computer.

 Exercise

>Decide which apps you will use for time management, health tracking, and financial records.

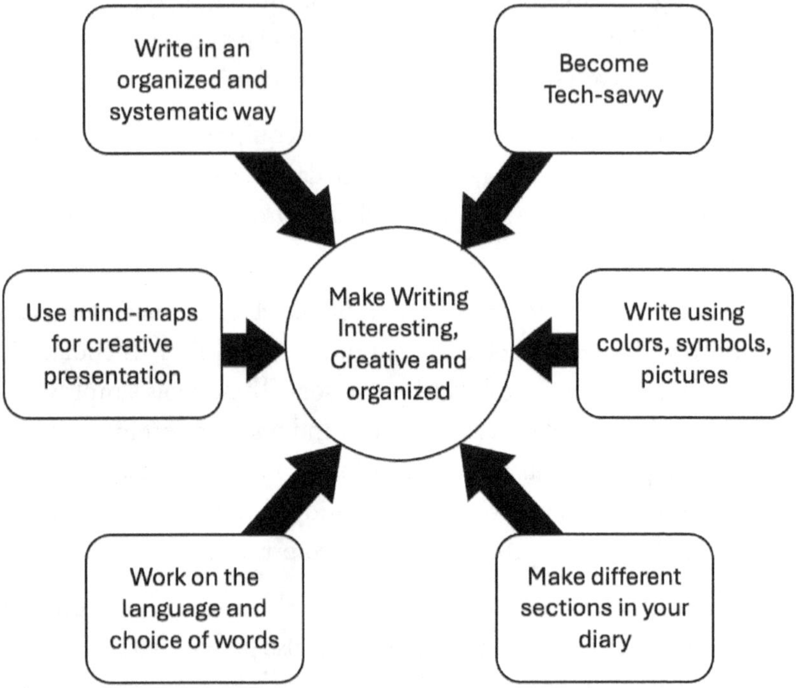

```
                    ┌─────────────┐              ┌─────────────┐
                    │ Write in an │              │   Become    │
                    │organized and│              │ Tech-savvy  │
                    │systematic way│             │             │
                    └──────┬──────┘              └──────┬──────┘
                           ↓                            ↓
┌──────────────┐         ╭─────────────────╮         ┌──────────────┐
│Use mind-maps │         │  Make Writing   │         │ Write using  │
│ for creative │ ──────→ │  Interesting,   │ ←────── │colors, symbols,│
│ presentation │         │  Creative and   │         │   pictures   │
└──────────────┘         │    organized    │         └──────────────┘
                         ╰─────────────────╯
                           ↑                            ↑
                    ┌─────────────┐              ┌─────────────┐
                    │ Work on the │              │Make different│
                    │language and │              │sections in your│
                    │choice of words│            │    diary    │
                    └─────────────┘              └─────────────┘
```

 [3] - To know more, read the book *Mastering the Art of Time Management* - A Happy Thoughts Initiative.

Scan this QR code to order your copy.

15

Write to Plan

The secret of getting ahead is getting started.
~ Agatha Christie

Rahul was a promising student in his college. He wanted to pursue studies in the civil services. All his professors had high expectations of him. While his goal was evident from his speech, he struggled to articulate a clear plan when asked about his preparation strategy. Sometimes, he would mention taking coaching classes; other times, he would talk about self-study. He began evading questions to avoid scrutiny because he lacked a concrete action plan.

In reality, he was entangled in the web of his own thoughts. Despite having a clear goal, he could not progress due to the lack of a clear action plan. His mind kept pulling him in different directions, leading to more confusion.

As the deadline for filling out the application form approached, he found himself increasingly confused about his next steps. In this predicament, he sought advice from one of his professors. The professor advised him to write down his goal and the plan to achieve it.

Although Rahul was initially unsure about what to write, he followed his professor's advice and began writing. He started by noting down sequential information such as exam dates, available coaching classes, and how many study hours he would need to pass the exam. While gathering this information, he also learned that physical fitness was necessary for the exam.

Then he continued writing about how much time he had for studies, whether he could prepare for the civil services exam along with his college exams, and what percentage of marks he needed to secure admission comfortably.

As he wrote all this down, he gained clarity. His confidence grew as he realized that he still had time, and everything was possible with hard work. He enrolled in a nearby coaching class.

In this way, by writing down his goal and action plan, Rahul gained confidence and could easily implement his plan. He deduced that merely thinking about tasks was not enough; only when they were put into written form could they gain momentum and accelerate progress.

Rahul's example demonstrates that when the mind is full of thoughts, it tends to wander aimlessly in different directions, creating confusion. However, when these thoughts are verbalized, they gain strength. Moreover, when they are put on paper, the mind receives a definite action plan. This underscores the importance of written words.

Similarly, we often think about performing numerous tasks in the present, completing pending tasks from the past, and accomplishing potential tasks in the future. When these tasks merely remain as thoughts in our minds, they often remain unfinished. According to the Second Law of Writing, when we verbalize them, we gain the strength to accomplish them. Additionally, when we mindfully write them down, the chances of their completion increase significantly.

Therefore, discuss your tasks with someone and also write them down. Words written consciously are more potent than mere speech. Through writing, tasks become more manageable and are more easily accomplished.

Make a to-do list

You may have experienced that while you are busy doing numerous tasks throughout the day, countless other thoughts occur simultaneously. Sometimes, you might be engaged in one activity but also thinking about other activities that need to be completed. When you are overwhelmed with thoughts like, "I need to complete this task," "I need to attend to that work as well," and "When will I complete them," you become burdened with these thoughts, often even without realizing it.

The human brain is designed such that it can handle several thoughts at the same time. These thoughts only exist in the mind and have no separate existence. Since the mind is never stable, thoughts keep arising and subsiding. Therefore, thinking can be considered rough work here. When the same thoughts are transferred on paper, they gain a separate and more solid existence. They can then be called fair work. Similarly, as long as the thoughts about tasks are in the mind, they are akin to rough work. When they are written down as a to-do list, they get transformed into fair, actionable items.

You might have experienced that many times during the day, you think about performing some tasks, remembering to tell someone something or calling someone, and so on. But since you have not written these thoughts and are busy in your daily routine, these thoughts slip away from your mind. Later, you struggle to recall those thoughts and the activities. Therefore, strive to be always aware of your thoughts related to any tasks. As soon as you think about any task, write it down on paper or record it on your smartphone. If you fail to record it on time and just try to memorize it, there is every possibility of forgetting and thus losing it.

Therefore, if you find it difficult to write down your long-term plans, you can start by writing down your daily tasks. The to-do list is a simple technique for organizing personal and professional tasks. By making and regularly updating a to-do list, you can focus on your activities and complete them on time.

Let us understand how and when to make a to-do list.

1. Daily list for the next day

Before going to bed at night or whenever you find time during the day, list the tasks to be done the next day. The following day, check the tasks that have been completed and that are pending. Add the pending tasks to the next day's list.

2. Weekly or fortnightly lists

If you find it difficult to write down the tasks daily, you can make a to-do list for a week or a fortnight. Homemakers can include their domestic activities along with the tasks of their interest in their to-do list. Children can add their study time, play time, or time for meeting friends.

3. Holiday planning

You can also write down your holiday plan. This will help you maintain positive energy while completing your weekly activities. You will look forward to the break after working for the entire week.

4. Monthly tasks

Some tasks like grocery shopping recur monthly. You can make their list once because most of the things you require are the same every month. This will save the time spent on making a list every month. Similarly, take note of the date of payment of utility bills, children's school fees, salaries of the maid, driver, house help, etc. Once you have made a list of all these tasks, you just need to tick them off every time you complete them.

5. Set reminders

After making the list, you can set reminders on your smartphone, laptop, or tablet device. This way, within a few days, you will learn the art of saving your time and energy through time management. You will also be able to find time for your favorite activities that you have always wanted to pursue for a long time but couldn't due to a lack of time.

6. Small goals in free time

You can also take up small goals and work on them in your free time. This will give you a feeling of fulfillment. You can distribute the tasks according to their priorities, which will help reduce stress, boost confidence, improve quality, and enhance time management, thus making it easy to attain your goals. By doing tasks sequentially, you can become a good organizer.

 Exercise

Create To-do lists for your daily, weekly, and monthly tasks by referring to the format given below.

Today's tasks		This week's tasks	
Personal tasks	Official tasks	Personal tasks	Official tasks
1	1	1	1
2	2	2	2
3	3	3	3
4	4	4	4
5	5	5	5

Monthly tasks		
Tasks	Date	Yes/No
1. Electricity Bill	10th	
2. Mobile Bill	10th	
3. Internet Bill	15th	
4. Maid's Salary	2nd to 3rd	
5. Grocery shopping	4th to 6th	
6.		
7.		

There could be some more tasks you cannot set a time for. Whenever you find free time between tasks, you can use that to complete such activities. However, you need to note them in your Future Diary. We will understand about the Future Diary in the next topic.

Creating a future diary of activities

Imagine how you would feel if you were told, "You have no work to do; just relax."

Naturally, you would feel good to hear that you only need to rest, especially since you are usually occupied with work all day. Not a day goes by when you have nothing to do—and now, just relax, no tasks, no to-do's, nothing! Just eat, sleep, and relax! But is it possible to live this way? How many days could you go without doing anything? Two days, four days, or maybe a week? Eventually, you would start looking for something to do because both your mind and body cannot stay idle.

Most people have become accustomed to being busy all the time. They find it difficult to remain idle, to just be by themselves. As soon as one task is completed, they move on to the next. Moreover, they want to complete all their future tasks today, but that is impossible. So, they carry the stress of those tasks. Often, people don't have a lot of work in the present but feel burdened by future tasks, thinking there just is not enough time for everything.

Whether it is the CEO of a company, a manager, or anyone else, the mere thought that "There is too much work to be done" always keeps people stressed and anxious. Some tasks are meant for the future, but they still occupy their mind, leading to mental fatigue that comes from simply thinking about the workload. This fatigue stems from the fear of forgetting some tasks or not being able to do them properly.

"What if I forget to do it on time?!" "What if I am unable to do it?!" "What if I do not have the ability or expertise to do it?!" "What if someone else does it before and better than me?!" This causes mental and even physical exhaustion!

Saying, "I have a lot of work," energizes one's thoughts, but until the thoughts are transformed into action, the restlessness remains. This is like someone racing their car while it is in neutral gear—too much energy without any movement. When energy is not properly channeled, the mind tends to become discouraged and torpid due to exhaustion.

From now on, when your mind feels burdened by future tasks, create a separate section in your diary and write down all such tasks you need to do in the future. These tasks need be done, though there is no strict deadline for them. For example, cleaning your closet, organizing important documents, buying items for your home or yourself, talking to certain people, etc. These tasks may not seem important at first glance, but they still need to be done. You can also include tasks you plan to do in 1, 3, or 5 years.

Call this section the FD or Future Diary. Just like a Fixed Deposit (FD), where you save money for future use, in a Future Diary, you list all your future tasks so that when you have free time or when you have finished your to-do list for the day, you can pick a task from this FD. This way, these tasks will gradually get done without requiring separate time or effort. Creating a Future Diary will clear your mind of the clutter of pending tasks. Otherwise, constantly thinking about tasks can be stressful, making even small tasks seem daunting.

Remember, as long as tasks remain circling in the mind, they will feel more intimidating. It is like standing at the foot of a mountain and looking up at its summit—of course, it will appear huge and overwhelming! But even the highest of mountains have been scaled in stages. That is what you do when you list down tasks on paper. Firstly, because you have quantified the abstract thought of "too many tasks," it will stop scaring and worrying you. Secondly, you now have a game plan to conquer the mountain!

When your mind gets boggled by thoughts of future tasks, write them in your FD and tell yourself, "I have no tasks at the moment; all tasks are for the future. I have written them down, and they will be done at the right time. So, I am free from worrying about them." This will relieve the stress of pending tasks, giving you a sense of freedom. With this sense of freedom, pick a task from your FD and start working on it. You will soon notice that the freedom you feel within also greatly enhances the quality of work.

Tasks done with a calm and unburdened mind gain a magical momentum. Work gets done smoothly and effortlessly; and before you know it, it is finished! You will be surprised at how much you have accomplished without realizing it. This is the secret you must uncover, where there is freedom from the stress of tasks, you are working on your tasks but are relaxed, and your tasks are getting done smoothly!

 Exercise

Create a Future Diary by referring to the format given below.

	Tasks for this year	Tasks for 3 years later	Tasks for 5 years later
1			
2			
3			
4			
5			

16

Write to Record and Remember

Write while the heat is in you. The writer who postpones the recording of his thoughts uses an iron which has cooled to burn a hole with.
-Henry David Thoreau

In the ancient Indian Gurukul system, knowledge flowed from Guru to disciple through oral tradition. Wisdom was imparted through recitation, passing it down across generations. Yet, over time, some of this knowledge faded or was distorted in its transmission.

The Buddha's teachings were initially passed down orally, as writing was not deemed essential then. As a result, some of this knowledge was lost over the years. Later, his disciples inscribed his teachings in the Pali language, creating the Tripitaka.

Centuries later, Emperor Ashoka renounced war to seek peace in spiritual wisdom and embraced the Buddha's teachings as his guiding light. To ensure their preservation for future generations, he had these teachings engraved in stone across his empire, safeguarding them from distortion or being erased. This act solidified Buddhism as a lasting heritage, benefitting all. While oral traditions allowed the Buddha's knowledge to evolve, its preservation in writing ensured its permanence. It is owing to the miracle of writing that we can still see these teachings inscribed in stone, guiding people in every aspect of life.

The Vedas and Puranas, written centuries ago, are a rich reservoir of knowledge about Indian ethos and tradition. They are a window into the soul of India's heritage. Without these written records, understanding the diverse facets of India's religious, economic, social, spiritual, and cultural

 life would be daunting. Our written heritage illuminates every aspect of our lives, connecting us to our past.

Whether the ancient Vedas and Puranas or the inscriptions carved by Emperor Ashoka, they have endured through the ages because writing is easier to preserve. These texts have guided and inspired people for centuries. Like a lighthouse in a storm, writing acts as a beacon, lighting the way to a fulfilling life and preparing us to face any challenge.

When something is written, it provides a timeless glimpse into the ideology, knowledge, and thoughts of its era. Writing is a powerful tool for preserving and passing on knowledge without distorting its original meaning. What is inscribed stands the test of time, safeguarding the authenticity of our ideas, principles, and values as they are conveyed to future generations.

There was a time when we memorized words by repeatedly reciting and writing them. This technique ingrains words deeply in our minds, often for a lifetime. Most of us have experienced this. We continue to use words we learned in childhood, building our current vocabulary on that solid foundation.

Consider the evolution of transport and communication, from coal-powered trains to bullet maglev trains, and from vintage telephones to sleek smartphones. Without the original blueprints of these models preserved in written form, their journey to modernity would have been significantly longer. The early experiments and theories, meticulously documented in writing, paved the way for their refinement and upgrade.

All the inventions and modern equipment we see today are rooted in documentation and writing. Researchers, scientists, and engineers rely on deep reflection, existing resources, and meticulous note-taking to create or improve their work. By recording their experiments in detail, they ensure that future generations can access, recreate, and enhance their discoveries.

Another significant stride attributed to writing was witnessed during the global pandemic. As the world shifted online, from sales to education, many authors seized the opportunity to write and promote eBooks. Writing and publishing evolved with this digital shift, and the dip in the number of readers and writers worldwide was recovered by a re-kindled interest in books.

Writing to remember

"Many of life's failures are people who did not realize how close they were to success when they gave up."
~Thomas Edison

"Perseverance is not a long race; it is many short races one after the other."
~ Walter Eliot

Have you ever noticed a sign with quotes like the ones mentioned above as you walked down the street?

You might have wanted to jot down that line but couldn't because you were in a hurry. Sometimes, you encounter touching words or inspiring sentences you wish to remember or even recite immediately. Yet by the time you get home, they are only half-remembered. And you think, "I wish I had written it down."

This happens to almost everyone—you see, hear, or read something memorable, but later, it slips away. If you had written it down, it would have become a lasting part of your diary. For example, a professional who regularly notes inspiring quotes and ideas from books and seminars finds them enriching their presentations and boosting their career prospects. Similarly, someone who consistently writes down personal goals and reflections gains deeper insights, leading to positive changes in behavior and relationships.

Writing is a skill that improves with practice. If something you read or experience leaves a lasting impression, be sure to write it down.

In olden times, people often had the habit of writing things down. If they read something noteworthy in a book, they would immediately jot it down in their diary and revisit it later. Writing improves memory and increases the likelihood of retention. Once written down, it is effectively captured in your mind.

When a sentence is read repeatedly, it becomes ingrained in your subconscious mind. This might explain why people often reread inspiring biographies, adopting their principles and teachings into their lives. You may have noticed some readers using a pencil or marker to highlight important sentences while they read. Later, they reflect on those lines and write down their essence, revisiting them from time to time. This practice helps them understand and remember the material more easily. Some even write a synopsis of the book to refer to instead of rereading the entire text, finding it beneficial to review the synopsis in their free time.

Many businesspeople meticulously document their company's activities, significant events, and important decisions. They also record any relevant information they receive about their business, ensuring it is readily accessible when needed. This practice keeps them well-informed and helps them make better decisions.

Some people forget where they have placed an item and spend considerable time and energy searching for it. If this happens to you too, you can avoid the frustration by writing it down in your diary or taking a photo on your smartphone as soon as you put it away. This simple practice makes it easy to get it later.

Thus, keeping a written record of topics that interest you can be highly beneficial. If you have a specific area of interest, make sure to document the related information in writing.

17

Write to Ideate and Introspect

Writing is a calling, not a choice.
~ Isabel Allende

When a mobile service company first introduced the slogan, "The world at your fingertips," as part of its advertising campaigns, it seemed like a lofty promise. But today it is a reality. With a smartphone in hand, you can connect with anyone, anywhere, anytime. The world is truly in your hands!

It is hard to imagine the initial spark of inspiration that led to the invention of the smartphone. Surely, countless hours of research, experimentation, and meticulous documentation went into its creation. Since its invention to its current state-of-the-art form, the technology and features of the smartphone have constantly evolved. Its current form is a testament to human ingenuity and innovation.

The human mind is inherently designed to generate new ideas. It is up to each person to decide whether to write them down to catalyze the creative process or let them wither away. Some may fear that their ideas will be ridiculed or rejected or worry about failure. However, those who ignored such concerns and persevered with their new ideas often reached the pinnacle of success.

You might wonder what exactly ideas are. Ideas are essentially new thoughts that arise in your mind that you pursue with dedication. Sometimes, while working on a task, you might think, "Let me try this differently or in a new way and see how it turns out." This thought process reflects the continuous development of your brain. The more you use your brain, the more new ideas it generates. However, since you may not remember every new thought, it is essential to write them down.

New ideas keep your mind active and broaden your scope of thinking. Therefore, whenever a new idea emerges, jot it down immediately, regardless of what you are doing. Even if it seems irrelevant at first, it could prove invaluable later. So, never dismiss any idea as worthless. Even if you don't see an immediate use, continue to document them. Eventually, you will accumulate enough ideas that you will find something useful when you will need it. Regularly review your ideas to identify which ones might be relevant at any given time.

Whenever you need to create something new, put the idea on paper first. Writing makes it easier to understand and explain any concept effectively. When you support an idea with logic and put it into words, you also connect with its associated feelings. This alignment between head and heart fosters creative expression. Regular writing practice keeps your mind active and peaceful and enhances your creativity.

You may have noticed that creative ideas often come to you early in the morning when your mind is fresh and calm. These new thoughts, filled with imagination and innovation, inspire growth. Writing them down immediately is crucial, or they may get lost in the flood of mundane thoughts. That's why it is advised to write when your mind is calm, such as in the early morning or late at night when your surroundings are peaceful.

Nowadays, some people even charge money to share their ideas. However, this is possible only when you write down your ideas. Documenting your ideas helps you gain clarity and allows you to effectively explain them to others.

Writing down an idea makes it easier to read, analyze, evaluate, and communicate through contemplation and reasoning. Repeatedly reading about an idea reveals its different dimensions and uncovers hidden aspects that you may have overlooked initially. Besides communication and reasoning, writing also enhances analytical skills.

 Exercise

Out of the many recent ideas you have had, write down the ones you remember.

Write to introspect

In today's digital age, a lot of time is spent on social media indiscriminately. Instead, that precious time can be used to reflect on past experiences. Analyze what went well, what didn't, what you can do to address the issues that didn't go well. This introspection can help you find solutions to a range of life's problems, from minor to major. Similarly, outlining your plans for the next day, detailing how you will execute them, and envisioning the possible outcomes will prepare you better for what lies ahead. In this way, writing paves the way for your growth.

When you start writing, you give voice to your thoughts and emotions. By analyzing them from various perspectives, you gain clarity about your thoughts. Writing empowers your thinking and boosts your confidence. As you write, your past thoughts, knowledge, experiences, and lessons contribute to your future growth. In other words, writing down the lessons learned from past mistakes helps you introspect more effectively. Even on days when you don't feel like writing, taking the time to do so trains your brain to actively pursue results, fostering its development.

Humans are social beings, and the people around you, like your neighbors, relatives, friends, and family members, form an integral part of your life. You experience many ups and downs in life, during which people around you play their roles. Just as in a play, the story advances through the interplay of many characters, the story of life unfolds when people play different roles, like that of parents, siblings, in-laws, spouses, children, and so on.

Everyone contributes to the story, whether positively or negatively. However, while playing the roles, they may get so entangled in the story that they hold on to certain feelings in their hearts. In the drama of life, some people speak lovingly, some praise, some offer help, and some may become angry or arrogant. But regardless of these experiences, the play of life goes on.

Now, write down all these incidents of your life and find ways to grow from them. Engage in creative activities so that the drama of life brings you joy instead of sorrow.

Every day, write down the incidents in your life and how you reacted to them. For instance, if someone asked you to do something and you agreed but still failed, analyze the reason behind it. Did you genuinely want to do it but could not for some reason, or did you say "yes" just for the sake of it, without actually intending to do it? Write down these details thoroughly.

Reflect on: "What am I saying? How am I saying it? Am I being straightforward or beating around the bush? Am I saying what should be said first, or am I saying what should be said later? What is my hidden intention behind it?"

Write down all these minute details, and when you read them again, you will understand whether your actions were truly right or whether they were hindering your growth. When you gain the right understanding through introspection, you will be ready to change yourself. Otherwise, these thoughts will stay in your mind and continue to entangle you. When your heart and mind feel burdened, new paths stop opening up, either slowing down or halting your growth. Therefore, learn to assess your true nature through reflective writing and steer your life in a positive direction.

Let us understand this with an example. A schoolteacher struggled to remember the students' names, making it challenging to recall who was bright, who was weak in studies, who was mischievous, and who often missed school. To address this issue, the teacher devised a creative solution. He created an alphabetical list of all the students' names and noted down their strengths and the guidance they needed. The teacher kept this list in his pocket, and whenever he had time, he would read it to remember the names and think about how best to guide each student.

Besides this, the teacher also devised new ways for disciplining students who made mistakes. Once the names were remembered, the teacher also became familiar with the students' faces. Whenever students misbehaved or failed to complete their homework, the teacher would punish them according to their nature and ask them to do something new and creative. With this innovative disciplining approach, the teacher soon earned the students' admiration. They began participating in the class more attentively. This, in turn, boosted the teacher's ability to generate new ideas, which he wrote down and applied as needed, like new ways of filling out forms or memorizing lessons, etc. This fostered his personal growth and also contributed to the students' growth. This could become possible only because the teacher wrote down all his new ideas and used them effectively.

Similarly, it would help to write down the strengths and virtues of your family members, relatives, friends, and acquaintances to help improve your relationships.[4]

	Name	Relationship	Their qualities
1			
2			
3			
4			
5			

Remember, relationships are opportunities for mutual growth. Use them as a ladder for your development. Implement strategies to ensure that these relationships are not a burden but open pathways for your progress.

[4] - To know more, read the book *Celebrating Relationships* by Sirshree.

Scan this QR code to order your copy.

18

Write to Communicate

You write to communicate to the hearts and minds of others what's burning inside you, and we edit to let the fire show through the smoke.
~ Arthur Plotnik

Albert Einstein once said, "If you can't explain it simply, you don't understand it well enough."

When you thoroughly understand something and believe in it, you can easily express and implement it in your life with confidence. However, if your mind is not convinced about it, you hesitate to communicate it to others. You wonder, "How can I explain its benefits to others when I'm not convinced?"

Working on an idea without fully understanding or believing in it is even more challenging. If you intend to use that idea for your growth, how can you turn it into a stepping-stone without firm conviction?

Writing is an effective way to convey your thoughts, experiences, and messages to others. Whether through instant messaging apps, greeting cards, letters, emails, reports, or social media, writing allows you to express your thoughts and intentions in both personal and professional fields.

All people are interconnected through their thoughts and emotions. While you can easily communicate your thoughts through writing, your emotions remain invisible and can only be felt. You can convey them to some extent through words and directly communicate with some people, but you might find it difficult to communicate them with others. At such times, you must write them down first to communicate effectively.

In the past, people wrote letters to check on others' well-being, share news, and express their thoughts and feelings. At the end of their letters, they would write, "Please forgive me for any mistakes or hard feelings." This way, they conveyed their emotions and sought forgiveness if their words hurt the other person intentionally or unintentionally. This was a method of communicating[5] their feelings.

However, times have changed. Today, emails and instant messages have largely replaced letters and telegrams, and typing has replaced writing with a pen. A small smartphone accomplishes all your tasks through emails, messaging apps, and other digital platforms, offering the fastest communication method. As soon as you compose a message, your smartphone can instantly convey your thoughts and feelings to the other person, and you receive replies just as quickly. Gone are the days of waiting for weeks or days for a response.

With the advent of smartphones, writing has become incredibly convenient. Whether in a train, car, flight, or home, you can easily write using your smartphone, even if you don't have a paper, pen, or diary. Digital technology has simplified writing immensely. Additionally, social media platforms allow you to send messages to many people simultaneously and engage in written communication effortlessly. This era of seamless communication has made the world a smaller place.

Expressing emotions in relationships

Rahul and Seema were siblings who shared a close and loving bond. They lived in different cities. Rahul had some meetings in Seema's city. So, he called her.

> Rahul: "I'm coming over tomorrow."
> Seema: "Oh, I have a seminar all day tomorrow."
> Rahul: "No problem. You'll be back by evening, right?"
> Seema: "Yes."
> Rahul: "Just let me know where the keys will be."
> Seema: "Alright! I'll check with the neighbor to see if she'll be home tomorrow and then call you back."

After speaking with the neighbor, it was arranged that the keys would be with her. Seema left hurriedly for the seminar the next day and forgot to inform Rahul. She had to switch off her mobile phone at the seminar.

You can imagine what would have happened with Rahul. He couldn't contact Seema. Annoyed, he ended up staying at a hotel, assuming that either his sister didn't want him to stay over, or her husband didn't approve of it. If Seema had sent a brief message, it could have prevented the misunderstanding and avoided any resentment in their relationship.

Relationships help us share our feelings. Language serves the same purpose, enabling us to communicate our feelings effectively.

In today's digital age, everyone can easily communicate with each other at any time. However, just as a lack of communication can sometimes cause problems, sometimes hastily sending messages without a second thought can lead to misunderstandings. People often impulsively send whatever comes to their mind using messaging apps without considering how their words might be interpreted.

Though we can write our thoughts in words, we cannot always express our emotions effectively because words have limitations. People use only the words they know, but the meaning of these words can vary for others. For example, what one person sees as a "6" might be perceived as a "9" by another from the other side, leading to a misunderstanding. Therefore, it is crucial to express feelings along with words in relationships.

When we share our feelings, we start connecting with others. However, expressing feelings using the right words can often be challenging. We must delve deep into our emotions and use words that emanate from within to connect more deeply in relationships.

Sometimes, you may want to express your feelings and tell someone their words or behavior hurt or troubled you. However, you may lack the courage or hesitate, fearing that expressing yourself may lead to misunderstandings and damage the relationship. This situation can be quite complex. You can neither express your feelings nor remain quiet without expressing them. In such a situation, whatever you want to say, write it politely and lovingly and send it. Writing gives you space and time to reflect on what and how to communicate, which helps calm your mind and allows you to convey your message clearly in apt words.

While writing, keep a few points in mind:

1. Write with understanding. Avoid writing directly, "You did something wrong, and I was hurt." Instead, you can write, "I know that you did not intend to hurt or upset me, but I was affected by your behavior. I will try my best to understand your perspective better in the future and hope you will do the same." In this way, you will be able to understand the other person while also clarifying your point.

2. Be sure to clarify your intentions in writing. You can write, "My intention has never been wrong; I have never intended to hurt you."

3. Also, write about the other person's qualities and acknowledge how important they are in your life. Highlighting their strengths makes them feel valued and appreciated. They feel that you are sincere, value them, and have also understood them. Then, they also start understanding and valuing you in return.

4. You can seek forgiveness and express gratitude in writing, so the other person feels secure and comfortable and takes the necessary steps to bridge the gap.

Remember, whenever you communicate in writing, write in such a manner that even if someone else reads it, there will be no issues.

Another important benefit of writing is that when someone receives a letter, they have ample time to read it without reacting immediately. In contrast, when you speak directly, the other person may react impulsively, leaving you little opportunity to continue the conversation. A written letter lets them read and process your words calmly, facilitating better understanding.

Thus, when you cannot express your feelings verbally, conveying them through writing is an excellent alternative. People who have used this approach often find it very effective in bringing harmony and strength to their relationships. Written communication can help resolve misunderstandings, mend relationships, foster harmony, and improve relationships.

Written communication in business

Writing is a valuable tool for communicating, not only with family members but also in the professional world. Imagine you are a CEO, a manager, or a bank officer, and you need to give instructions to your employees or assistants. It is always better to provide those instructions in writing. When you give out instructions verbally, there is a chance of being misunderstood, which can lead to errors. However, when everything is written and documented, all the details are clear and can be reviewed later. Plus, written instructions can be kept as evidence if needed in the future.

These days, online meetings have become a powerful way to share work more deeply with colleagues. You can use graphs, presentations, and pictures to showcase your work. People can communicate from their respective locations simultaneously. One of the perks of online communication is that you can see each other's faces, read their expressions, understand their points more easily, and take notes during the discussion effortlessly.

The above points are common in business interactions. However, people often fail to express their feelings to others during work. For instance, if a boss appreciates an employee's or assistant's work and notices their qualities, he might not express it, fearing that praise might make them complacent. But often, the opposite is true; receiving praise can motivate them to work harder. Therefore, if you feel appreciative about someone at your workplace, do express it. This will encourage employees and help them work with dedication. If you find it hard to express verbally, written communication can help. You can convey it through a messaging app or an email.

For example, a mental hospital dean selected a senior nurse from his staff to handle a challenging case.

The dean told her, "You have a fantastic opportunity. This new case has never been seen in this hospital."

The nurse was excited, "Wow Sir, what do I need to do?"

The dean explained, "You need to care for this patient day and night and treat them compassionately."

The nurse, slightly apprehensive, said, "That will be very difficult, Sir!"

The dean reassured her, "I have confidence in your ability, and I believe you can do it well."

Hearing these words, the nurse felt a surge of pride and a passion for showcasing her abilities. Using her many years of experience, she compassionately devoted herself to her work. She performed her duties diligently and met the dean's expectations by caring for the patient. As a result, the hospital's reputation also improved. The dean, pleased with her work, honored her with a certificate of appreciation in front of the hospital staff. He read a letter he had written in her appreciation, which made the nurse feel proud and set an example for others.

Similarly, in every profession, when people appreciate and thank each other in writing, it leads to development and brings about a change of heart. Writing is a very effective medium for communicating emotions.

[5] - To know more, read the book *Mastering the Art of Communication* - A Happy Thoughts Initiative.

Scan this QR code to order your copy.

19

Write in the Air

If I waited for perfection, I would never write a word.
~ Margaret Atwood

Writing has become increasingly difficult nowadays because people have lost their habit. They come up with excuses to put off writing until another time.

You may have heard the story of the lion and the fox. A lion cub had lost its family and mistakenly begun to live with some foxes. It soon adopted the foxes' ways and started to behave like one. But one day, when it saw its own reflection in the water, it realized it was a lion, not a fox. Realizing that it was actually a powerful creature, its way of living completely changed.

Similarly, we have forgotten what it is to write. But, like the lion, restarting it once again will become easier when we remember that we already had the habit of writing when we all studied at school. We need to get back to the habit of writing again.

Many times, we do want to write. But despite our will, we often cannot maintain continuity in writing because lethargy overpowers us. At such times, if we use a new writing technique called Writing in the air, it can bring miraculous results.

You may have seen that some children, while doing math, move their fingers in the air while calculating mentally. Similarly, when a musician sets a tune, they first try to build a rhythm with their fingers along with the lyrics in their mind.

In this technique, whatever you wish to write, write it with your fingers so that even if written in the air, it can reach your subconscious mind and bring the same results as writing on paper. Although you are writing with gestures, it is not visible to anyone.

Some people use this technique to safeguard themselves from negative thoughts or incidents. For instance, if negative thoughts arise within them or they see any adverse situation, they say "Cancel, Cancel, Cancel," so they remain unaffected. However, some people just mark a cross in the air instead of saying "Cancel, Cancel, Cancel," and get the same result. Thus, marking a cross in the air once is easier than saying, "Cancel, Cancel, Cancel."

You can also use this technique to nurture positive thoughts or virtues and attract what you want in life. For example, on seeing an inspiring incident or something you have always wanted, you can gesture a tick (✓) in the air indicating to Nature: "This is something I want in my life." Just a tick in the air can do wonders!

Whatever things you want in your life or the desired results you are looking for, you can communicate to Nature by writing it in one word or symbol in the air.

H.E.A.L.T.H

For example, when you visit a hospital to see someone, you wish for their wellbeing. At such times, quietly write the letters H E A L T H in the air to communicate to Nature for the wellbeing of everyone present in the room.

However, if you feel awkward writing it in the air in front of people, simply fold your arms and write with your fingers in small letters unseen to everyone. You can also write it on the hand of the person you are visiting.

Whenever you feel lonely, you can write "Love" or "Joy" in the space of your room. This will permeate positive vibes in your space and within yourself. You can also use other words like "Forgiveness," "Bliss," "Peace," "Contentment," "Acceptance," or any words of your choice. These small words may seem insignificant, but their effect can be significant.

If some words are long, you can write their short form. For example, nowadays, people write "GM" to say, "Good morning." Similarly, whatever you want to achieve in your life, develop the habit of writing it in a few words or abbreviations.

As children, we wrote anywhere, be it on walls, shreds of paper, slate, or elders' notebooks. Wherever we saw a pen or pencil, we would write. Ironically, we scold our children for doing what we once did. But think about it. What a great gift we have received from Nature! Every child enjoys writing just about anywhere. They want to write what they learn. In the same spirit, let us make the entire sky our slate and write on it with our fingers as much as we want.

20

The 21-day Challenge of Daily Writing

I can shake off everything as I write;
my sorrows disappear, my courage is reborn.
~ Anne Frank

In the Bhagavad Gita, Lord Krishna states that the final stage of true awakening happens when wisdom translates into practical action. Often, people act out of ignorance. It is essential to gain the right understanding of karma. However, it is even more important to consistently put this understanding into practice. To elevate the quality of your karma, perform actions without attachment to the fruit. This is called *Nishkaam Karma* (desireless deeds).

Children learn the alphabet naively at school, unaware of the big picture. As they gain understanding, they begin to use letters to form simple words, such as "A for Apple" or "B for Ball." With practice, they learn to construct words and eventually use these words to create sentences, essays, and literature, marking the culmination of their karma of writing.

Similarly, practice writing a few lines daily, even if it is just for 5 minutes. Ensure to sit consistently for those 5 minutes every day for 21 days without a break. It doesn't matter what you write during that time. It is important to spend that time with pen and paper without focusing on the number of words or pages you write.

By sitting at the designated time regularly, you signal to Nature that you are open to receive guidance for your writing process. You must show your commitment. Set an alarm for your designated writing time and see what happens after 21 days! If you miss a day, consider the next day as the first day and start the 21-day challenge again. Ensure you maintain this rhythm throughout the 21 days.

According to neuroscience, performing any activity consistently for 21 days wires it into your brain, turning it into a habit. Likewise, practicing writing for 21 consecutive days makes it a habit. Once you start the challenge and sit regularly at the designated time, something will emerge, possibilities will unfold, and results will begin to materialize.

According to the First Law of Writing, "Writing bridges the visible and invisible forms of karma, speeding up the manifestation of its outcome and the resulting feelings." Just as raindrops, though small, can fill vast rivers and lakes when they fall continuously, every small effort of writing can lead to a significant transformation in life.

 Plan of action

When will you begin the 21-day writing challenge?

....

How long will you sit for writing? .... minutes

Time (morning, evening, night): .... to ....

The place where you will sit: ....

Which diary or book will you use? ....

PART 4

THERAPEUTIC WRITING

21

Write to Heal

*By writing down your negative emotions,
they begin to weaken immediately.
When they are brought to light, their power ends.*

Our life is a journey filled with countless events. Despite our will, some of these events can disrupt our peace and cause turmoil.

Imagine sitting calmly by a river, gazing at your reflection. Suddenly, a leaf floats by, or a child throws a pebble into the still water. Your reflection shimmers and becomes distorted. Thus, even a single pebble can create ripples on the calm water surface. Similarly, a single incident can alter the course of your smoothly running life.

Every thought or word carries positive or negative energy. When you write these thoughts down, their energy permeates the environment. Positive thoughts transmit positive energy, eventually strengthening all the positive energies of the universe. Conversely, writing about negative experiences can initially intensify negative emotions. However, once written in detail on paper, these negative emotions begin to dissipate, allowing positive energies to emerge within. This process helps heal negative emotions as nature is inherently positive.

Many people often harbor emotions like anger, envy, hatred, and malice, which are reflected in their responses. However, when they begin writing these emotions on paper, these emotions gradually begin to fade away.

For example, Raman used to struggle with anger. Whenever he got angry, he would lash out at others with abusive language. Despite his best intentions, he would lose his temper and say things he would regret later. To overcome this tendency, he began writing down every incident of anger, including the hurtful words he used. This exercise provided a sense of catharsis, allowing him to confront his anger. By examining his written accounts, he gained a deeper understanding of his triggers. Over time, he became more aware during the bouts of anger and avoided using abusive language. Gradually, he freed himself from anger and achieved healing.

The practice of writing dates back centuries. Many people used to keep personal diaries. It has been observed that when someone consistently writes down their experiences, transformative changes begin to happen in their life. Writing imbues words with power, making them manifest into reality.

In essence, writing serves as a therapeutic practice that helps maintain mental well-being. It helps you heal and eliminate any tendency, habit, or pattern. Just as clearing out a cluttered closet can create space for new things, writing down old habits and tendencies can free the mind from the baggage of the past, allowing new ideas and creative energy to emerge. You will feel inspired to try something new, your perspectives will shift, and you will begin to see the world with a new positive lens. This process of self-reflection facilitates healing.

Liberation from negative memories[6]

In a study involving individuals with deep-seated negative memories, participants were asked to write about their experiences, both good and bad. Some wrote about their painful experiences, while others only wrote about their future plans, avoiding sharing their distress. Those who wrote about their pain became free from those hurtful memories and associated thoughts, whereas those who did not write continued to endure the same suffering and distress. With this study, the researchers found a profound connection between the mind and the body.

People often have memories buried deep within them for years, which they can neither share nor wish to remember. These memories can fester like a wound, overshadowing their personality or sometimes manifesting as physical or mental ailments. Writing can be a valuable and effective method for freeing oneself from such negative memories that may surface as mental health issues. It offers a chance to distance themselves from old memories. By writing them down, they transfer these events from their mind onto paper, allowing the wounds of years to begin healing. In this way, they can eradicate their bad experiences, fears, and shortcomings. Writing down negative emotions reduces stress levels and helps dissipate the negative energy stored in the body, leading to happiness, peace, and liberation.

A question often arises where and how to write down negative thoughts and emotions. It is best to write them in a way that allows you to erase them easily. It is important not to hold onto them. While significant negative experiences that taught you valuable lessons or positively changed the course of your life can be preserved, other negative experiences, such as insults, cheating, abuse, humiliation, fears, adverse incidents, and insecurities, should be written in a way that allows for easy erasure. They should leave no lasting impact on your life. Writing them on paper is recommended, as paper can be easily destroyed. By destroying the paper, you can symbolically release the negative emotions attached to those experiences.

After writing and releasing negative emotions, the mind then becomes free to receive the best that Nature offers. All the positive outcomes you have always aspired for, such as health, wealth, love, prosperity, happiness, and progress, come into your life.

Research from the University of Oslo in Norway indicates that writing can enhance mental, physical, and emotional well-being. James Pennebaker, author of "Writing to Heal," asserts, "Writing makes you emotionally strong, and this improves your immune system."

Here are some suggestions for freeing yourself from negative thoughts and emotions, releasing harmful tendencies and limiting patterns from within. By adopting these practices, you can let go of the beliefs holding you back, allowing yourself to heal old wounds that you have been carrying, mistakenly believing them to be true.

1. Write down the thoughts that trouble and sadden you on paper. Then, release them by attaching the paper to a kite and flying it into the sky. As you do this, visualize yourself releasing all your negative thoughts and emotions into the universe, feeling completely free from them.

2. You may have seen children playfully making paper boats and floating them on water. You can do the same to release negativity symbolically. Write down all your limiting or negative beliefs on paper, fold it into a boat, and let it float away in a stream, river, or any body of water. As the boat drifts away, imagine all your sorrows, dilemmas, and pains floating away.

3. Historically, a sacred fire pit, known as the *Havan Kund*, was used for worship in temples and ashrams, where the environment would get purified, eliminating all negative energies. You can emulate this practice by writing down all your negative emotions on separate slips of paper and offering them into a fire, accompanied by the invocation "*Swaha*." Visualize you are becoming free of all negative energies with every invocation.

4. You can also express your emotions through drawings with crayons or coloring pens. Draw pictures representing your negative thoughts and emotions, and then dispose of them however you choose.

Writing down feelings of despair, sorrow, negative memories, remorse, and guilt can help you release them and heal your past. Life gains meaning when you align with God's will, embrace divine qualities, and live in love, joy, and contentment.

 Exercise

1. Write five incidents that caused disappointment, remorse, anger, guilt, or sadness in your journal.

2. Now, cross out the incidents you listed (XXXXX) feeling that these negative aspects are being erased from your life.

 [6] - To know more, read the book *Heal Your Memories, Heal Your Life* by Sirshree.

Scan this QR code to order your copy.

22

Heal False or Limiting Beliefs

The art of writing is the art of discovering what you believe.
~ Gustav Flaubert

Many of the practices and rituals we follow today were initiated by our ancestors. While times have changed, we continue to adhere to these traditions, often without fully understanding their original intent and purpose. Although we sometimes feel troubled by these practices, we often lack the curiosity to explore their meaning or the courage to challenge them. When asked why we follow these traditions, we simply say, "Our elders followed them and instructed us to do so, so we do it." We respect their guidance and, therefore, follow these practices without doubt or debate.

While some old beliefs fade away, new beliefs take their place. For instance, there are many beliefs about technology and lifestyle, such as "Having every luxury and convenience equals true happiness," "Life is short, so why save for the future? Live for today and enjoy life now!" Whether a belief is old or new, it remains just a belief. Its truth or falsity depends on each individual's level of understanding[7].

However, these beliefs have become empty notions over time, and their underlying truth has lost its significance. For example, some people believe that "Money is the root of all evil" or "Wealth is fleeting." But is this true? Some people possess great wealth, while others struggle financially. Some squander their money, while others save diligently.

Thus, these beliefs affect each one differently. Beliefs without logic or truth are merely empty notions that people cling to.

The truth, however, is universal and consistent. For instance, the nature of water is wetness. The moon orbits the Earth, and the Earth orbits the sun. The moon's gravity influences the ebbs and tides of the seas. Every person goes through childhood, youth, old age, and death. Every living being breathes. These are truths that remain constant and are true for everyone.

In contrast, beliefs vary depending on the person's upbringing, cultural influence, circumstances, and location. For instance, someone might believe, "Happiness is not in my destiny; no matter how hard I try, my life will always be filled with troubles and sorrow." However, this is not the truth! This belief can be changed. By speaking about it and writing it down, its energy can be channeled in a positive way.

Nisha was a well-educated girl working at a multinational company in a very good position, earning a good salary. Although she was of marriageable age, she struggled to find a suitable partner. Nisha and her parents believed that mutual respect in a married couple required the husband to be more educated and earn more than the wife. This belief led her to reject many promising proposals.

Nisha's friends advised her to let go of this belief and embrace a new perspective. She began to reflect in writing: "Instead of focusing on education and salary, it is more important to find a partner who is well-behaved, respectful, and of good character. We can pool our salaries together to manage the household effectively."

Through this written contemplation, Nisha also uncovered other deeply ingrained beliefs she held, such as the groom should be older, taller, and have a compatible horoscope. She realized that these beliefs were limiting her options and hindering her marriage. Instead, she should prioritize understanding, love, and trust in a marital relationship.

She realized that many of the beliefs she had assumed to be true were merely empty notions without any inherent truth. By writing them down, she could confront and release them. She began searching for a life partner with a renewed perspective.

Reflect on your life and identify the beliefs you hold as truths that cause you distress and sorrow. For example, beliefs like "Nobody values me or my ideas," "No one loves me," "I am unlucky" are often unfounded beliefs that need to be challenged and discarded. Start writing about them: "What beliefs have shaped my life so far? Why am I unhappy? How would my life be without these beliefs?"

To identify your beliefs, use this sentence structure: When ... happens, then ... will happen. For example, when I find a life partner, then I will be happy. When I have a certain bank balance, then people will value me.

Use this technique to even uncover your deeply ingrained beliefs. These beliefs are buried deep within and rarely come to the surface. Therefore, people seldom reflect on them deeply; even if they do, they do it in their minds, which can be misleading, especially when crowded with thoughts. The effective approach is to contemplate in writing.

As you continue to write, you will gain clarity from within. You will connect with your subconscious mind and discover the roots of these beliefs. Once you know the truth, letting go of these beliefs will become easier.

 Exercise

1. Write down at least five beliefs that cause you distress and sorrow.

2. Complete the sentence to identify the underlying beliefs.

Example: When <u>someone appreciates my work</u>, then <u>I will work sincerely</u>.

When <u>someone gives me an expensive gift</u>, then <u>I will feel loved</u>.

When .... happens, then..will happen.

 [7] - To know more, read the book *Everything is a game of beliefs, understanding is the whole thing* by Sirshree.

Scan this QR code to order your copy.

23

Attain Freedom from the Past

We write to taste life twice, in the moment and in retrospect.
~ Anais Nin

Life is a journey filled with ups and downs, joys and sorrows, gains and losses. These experiences are an integral part of life, allowing us to understand its rich tapestry. In the grand scheme of things, these experiences are temporary. Sorrow is often followed by joy, night turns into day, and problems come with solutions. Yet, sometimes, we are so engulfed in misery that we fail to see the opportunities and solutions right in front of us.

If a negative incident occurred in your past, don't escape or suppress it. Instead, face it and drive away the grief caused by it. Just as you won't let a stranger enter your home uninvited, don't let sadness or negative thoughts invade your mind. Take charge and actively dispel grief, destroying it instead of letting it drown you.

You might be familiar with the idiom, "Crush your enemies under your feet so they never rise again." Similarly, you must completely crush your sorrows under your feet, or they will find their way back into your life. Here is a creative way to free yourself from past pain. Take a marker and write down your troubling thoughts from the past on the soles of your shoes. Use acronyms or short forms like "J" for jealousy. If you want to be free from an illness, write its name or the first letter. Trust that as you walk, these problems will be crushed and destroyed.

Before you walk with the shoes on, touch the earth lovingly and say, "Dear Mother Earth, I love you. Fill me with love, joy, and peace. Dissolve all the grief, illness, and challenges written under my shoes, and free me from them. I am forever grateful to you. Thank you for bringing love, joy, and peace into my life."

Then, walk on the earth, holding the positive intention that as you walk the path of love, joy, and peace, your negative past is being scrubbed away forever. Remember, Mother Earth is ready to take away all your misery, so let go of everything that troubles you—the past, disease, fear, guilt, resentment, remorse, and limiting beliefs.

In this exercise, you can also decide a route to walk with these shoes. It is important to give this route a meaningful name. For instance, you can name your route to work, "Love and Joy." Write down the negative emotions you experience on the soles of your shoes and walk along this route, repeating "Love and Joy." Similarly, you can name your route to the market, "Peace and Patience", the route to a loved one's house, "Faith and Compassion," and so on. This way, by naming your regular routes, you can benefit from this exercise more frequently.

Writing is an effective way to free yourself from past memories. Your diary offers a private and safe space to express your thoughts and feelings openly. As you begin to write, you gain clarity on your emotions, challenges, and victories. Writing a diary helps you develop insights into your mind and understand your memories in a positive light. If practiced regularly, it brings inner peace, freedom, and mental upliftment.

 Exercise

List down negative thoughts and past events you will write on the bottom of your shoes in your journal.

24

The Healing Power of Storytelling

If a story is in you, it has to come out.
~ William Faulkner

There is a strange, almost paradoxical, healing power in written storytelling. When you repeatedly write about your own stories, especially the painful ones, you might initially experience a surge of emotions. Tears might flow, anger might boil, and fear might creep in. But as you continue to explore these feelings by writing them down, a curious transformation begins.

The intensity of the emotions gradually diminishes. The pain that once felt so raw and immediate starts to lose its edge. This isn't because you are becoming indifferent; rather, it is because you allow yourself to process and understand your emotions in a deeper way[8]. By confronting your pain head-on and giving it a voice, you can gradually desensitize yourself to its intensity.

The goal is to feel your emotions fully, to experience them without holding back. By repeatedly revisiting your painful experiences, you learn to accept them. You acknowledge that these experiences were a part of your life and have shaped your life course. As you come to terms with your past, you begin to let go of the emotional baggage that has been weighing you down.

Consider someone who has experienced a traumatic event. By writing about this event repeatedly, they might initially feel overwhelmed by feelings of fear, anger, and sadness. However, as they continue exploring these emotions through their writing, they might begin to notice patterns emerging. They might realize that certain thoughts or behaviors are contributing to their ongoing distress. By identifying these patterns, they can address them more effectively.

When someone struggling with guilt or regret starts writing about their past mistakes, they begin to understand the underlying reasons for their feelings. They might realize they were acting out of fear or insecurity rather than malice. By acknowledging their mistakes and forgiving themselves, they can begin to move forward.

Repetitive writing can serve as a powerful tool for healing. By confronting your painful experiences and giving them a voice through writing, you can begin to process your emotions in a healthy way. As you continue to explore your story, you may find that the intensity of your emotions gradually diminishes. While this might seem like a loss, it is actually a sign of healing. As you let go of your past pain, you are freeing yourself to live more fully in the present.

Writing about painful incidents repeatedly and reading and rereading your narratives can lead you to a profound realization: the futility of dwelling on the past. The exaggerated value you initially assigned to these events along with the intense emotions they stirred, gradually fades. You will begin to see the absurdity of holding onto grudges or lingering in pain.

Writing then becomes a therapeutic exercise to confront your emotional baggage head-on. As you pour your thoughts and feelings on paper, you gain new perspectives on your experiences. You see the patterns, the recurring themes, and how your past has shaped your present. Through this process, you begin to understand the root causes of your pain and how you can move beyond them.

A bird's-eye view

One of the most remarkable aspects of writing your own stories is the newfound perspective it grants you. When you are caught up in the heat of the moment, emotions can cloud your judgment and distort your perception of reality. But when you sit down to write about these experiences, you are forced to step back and examine them from a distance. It is like gaining a bird's-eye view of a landscape once obscured by fog.

As you write, you begin to see the bigger picture. You start to understand why certain characters in your story acted the way they did, even if their actions were hurtful or confusing at the time. You see the underlying motivations that drove their behavior, the fears and insecurities that shaped their choices. This newfound understanding can be both liberating and painful, but it is ultimately a necessary part of the healing process.

By re-examining your stories objectively as a detached witness, you can let go of your past judgments. You can see that your own biases and assumptions may have led you to misinterpret the intentions of others. You can recognize that people are complex beings, capable of both good and bad, and that their actions are often influenced by factors beyond their control.

Consider someone who has been betrayed by a friend. When they are initially hurt, they may be consumed by anger and resentment. They may feel that their friend has deliberately wronged them, and they may harbor feelings of hate and ill will. However, as they write about the incident, they may begin to see things from their friend's perspective. They may realize that their friend was perhaps going through a difficult time and that their actions were not intended to cause harm. This newfound understanding can help alleviate their anger and resentment and pave the way for forgiveness.

In essence, writing can help you to gain a new perspective on your past experiences. By stepping back and examining your stories from a distance, you can see the bigger picture and let go of your past judgments. This can be a powerful tool for healing and growth. Additionally, this process teaches you vital life lessons like patience, empathy, and resilience. You begin to appreciate how others have co-created in your life journey to bring you experiences that help you learn and grow.

Write your autobiography

You might have noticed that biographies of famous people are available because everyone wants to know about them. But are we equally curious about ourselves as we are about others? Probably not.

You may think that only famous people write their biographies and there is nothing special in your life worth writing about. However, everyone's life story is unique. Although an ordinary person's life might seem mundane, each person is the hero or heroine of their own life. Every person may appear similar on the outside, but each individual has unique qualities that make them special and distinct.

Until now, you have seen and remembered your life's events in fragments. Sometimes, during leisure, while talking to someone, or while recalling a memory, a particular incident comes to your mind, and you remember it. But now, try to read through the book of your life in its entirety. Remember your entire life all at once. Pick up a pen and start writing your life story, your autobiography.

Consider the following points to know what and how you will write before you begin.

- While writing, you might experience moments when your old emotions resurface. However, honestly write down your mental and emotional state as it is.

- When writing an autobiography, everyone writes about their common qualities. However, it is important to highlight your extraordinary qualities as well. Hence, focus more on them.

- Write about events that have significantly changed your life, opportunities that have highlighted your qualities, your growth, and the recognition you have received for your achievements. Confidently write about your experiences, knowledge, and ways to achieve goals that might inspire others.

- From childhood to the present, describe how you have faced challenges, achieved success, and worked in various areas of life, such as physical, mental, financial, social, and spiritual. Describe your plans and strategies that helped you fulfill your resolutions and goals. Write down all of this as this is the truth of the life you have lived.

- Be sure to write down your personality traits, dreams, reliable associates, and qualities. Creatively present your experiences and learnings to keep yourself engaged and excited while reading it.

People know a lot about each other, but if asked to tell something about themselves, they often hesitate, wondering what to say. Now, your autobiography will introduce you to yourself. It will allow you to know about your unique qualities. It will bring forth the good and bad traits hidden within you and allow you to recognize your inner feelings. By identifying and accepting these qualities, you will find ways to improve them, plan to achieve your dreams and become a better version of yourself.

 Exercise

Write your autobiography.

 [8] - To know more, read the book *Emotional Freedom through Wisdom* by Sirshree.

Scan this QR code to order your copy.

PART 5

TRANSFORMATIVE WRITING

25

Write to Reprogram Yourself

Scattering words on paper is easy, but compiling them with beautiful language is the art of writing.

Have you ever watched a potter skillfully shaping a pot on his wheel? He kneads the clay with great affection and meticulous care, places it on the wheel, spins it round and round, and molds it with gentle yet firm pats. It is as if he is infusing his feelings into the clay. No matter how long it takes to achieve the perfect form, he persists with unwavering dedication, patience, confidence, and consistency until his creation is complete. This process brings him immense joy.

Similarly, when you direct your positive feelings and thoughts into words and write them down, you can experience profound happiness every time you revisit and read what you have written. Through writing, you also converse with the invisible forces of Nature, shaping your future.

Thousands of years ago, the science of Ayurveda prescribed several medical practices, such as plastic surgery, organ transplants, etc., which are prevalent today. In 1865, Jules Verne wrote a book titled "From the Earth to the Moon," describing human travel to the moon. Since 1940, Isaac Asimov's stories discussed the concept of robots and the three laws of robotics, which we now see in tangible form. To summarize, many things written centuries ago have manifested today because Nature also works toward development in the unseen.

Everyone has the right to dream and achieve their aspirations. Nature wholly supports the fulfillment of each dream. Dreams that are written down manifest much faster than those that are not. Therefore, write down every dream in detail to turn it into reality. When you write something and it manifests, your belief in the power of writing is reinforced. When this happens consistently, you begin to write with greater conviction. This kind of writing can be called Transformative Writing.

Change your programming

Many beliefs get ingrained in our minds from childhood to adulthood, and we lead and shape our lives based on them. It is now time to break that programming. Let us understand how to write affirmations to change your programming.

When you buy a new computer or smartphone, some apps are pre-installed, while others you add based on your needs. Your body, mind, and intellect also function similarly. When a child is born, their body and brain are pre-equipped to perform certain tasks while they learn other tasks as they grow. These experiences get imprinted and programmed in their subconscious mind over time through repetition.

Just as a line drawn repeatedly in the same place forms a deep impression, your thoughts, whether positive or negative, become deeply ingrained in your subconscious during incidents. They function like the apps you use on your smartphones according to your needs. Your subconscious mind uses these patterns and reacts accordingly when similar situations arise.

For example, if you habitually focus more on the negative aspects of every incident, your emotions and thoughts will predominantly be negative. You might tend to see more shortcomings in people around you, find problems with every season, and generally criticize utility services and civic institutions. All this happens unknowingly due to the negative programming of your subconscious mind.

However, this programming can be changed. Just as you can delete software programs from your device, you can erase negative emotions, thoughts, and beliefs from your subconscious mind and replace them with positive ones. Writing positive words or sentences can shift your thoughts, gradually erasing old programming and making way for new, positive programming.

Let us understand this further with an example. Pramila was a simple girl from a village. She excelled in her studies and took a keen interest in household chores, loved helping others. She married Manoj, who lived in the nearby city. Being raised in an urban setting, Manoj considered himself more sophisticated and viewed Pramila as naive and unpolished. His constant taunts, along with the criticism from his family, began to undermine Pramila's confidence. She started feeling inadequate, believing she didn't know the ways of city life, didn't wear modern clothes, and that her in-laws disliked her. These repetitive negative thoughts, such as, "I'm not smart," and "No one likes me or talks to me" became deeply ingrained in her subconscious. As a result, Pramila became fearful of speaking to others. She always remained quiet and apprehensive.

Her father-in-law respected her a lot. One day, he spoke to her and insisted that she enroll in a personality development course. There, she learned about repeating affirmations—positive self-suggestions. Now, whenever she found free time, she would sit down to write: "I am smart. I like everyone, and everyone likes me. I am fearless and filled with courage and creativity." Gradually, this brought about a change in her.

Now, instead of being fearful and apprehensive, she began to exude a newfound confidence. She would talk to her father-in-law and sister-in-law in English. She would drive the car to the market, shop, and manage the household. In this way, she changed the programming in her subconscious with a little effort.

You might also have some negative programming within you, and some negative feelings could disturb you. To change these, you must repeatedly write down new thoughts to reprogram your subconscious mind. This change can be made at any stage of life.

Crafting and writing affirmations[9]

Everyone perceives life differently. For some, it is full of joy and vibrancy. For others, it is an endless prison sentence, filled with complaints like, "I have no choice but to live out my days. If sorrow is my fate, what can I do? My destiny is rotten and brings a new problem every day." They do not realize that Nature responds with "So be it" to whatever they say, making it come true. By repeating negative thoughts, they invite sorrows and hardships yet blame fate.

It is a law of Nature that whatever you describe gets prescribed in your life. Research today shows that you become or gain whatever you repeatedly think and speak. It has been proven that words have their own charge or energy. Whatever you say boomerangs into your life. Knowing the power of words, why spread negative words and invite negativity? Instead, use positive words to bring positivity to your surroundings.

To transform your life, become aware of negative thoughts and immediately convert them into positive ones. Use affirmative words or phrases repeatedly, and you will soon experience a shift in your emotions. This repeated positive self-talk can include words like love, happiness, gratitude, health, or any mantra.

You can wield the power of affirmations for personal development, health, and many other areas of life. Affirmations like "I am confident," "I am capable," "I am healthy," or "I deserve success" effectively invoke positive outcomes. Given below are some guidelines for crafting affirmations.

1. Select a meaningful aspect of life

Affirmations can be crafted toward specific goals or desired results. Consider the various aspects of your life—physical, spiritual, financial, mental, and social. What do you want to achieve in each of these areas? Which qualities and skills do you want to develop? Which habits do you want to break? How do you want your relationships with people to be? Which negative emotions or thought patterns do you need to change?

Reflect on these questions and start with one aspect to craft your affirmations. Some examples include: "I am brimming with perfect health and energy," "I am successful," "I am getting better every day," or "I am always surrounded by positive people."

2. Pick positive words

The words you choose for affirmations should inspire your confidence, energy, and positive feelings. Use optimistic words like love, joy, peace, hope, victory, patience, determination, capability, and success.

3. Keep it concise

Your affirmations should be short, simple, and clear so they are easy to write, remember, and repeat.

4. Use "I" and "my" to evoke positive feelings

Use personal pronouns in a positive light to give a clear indication to Nature. Pronouns like "I," "me," and "my" create a strong personal connection, making your affirmation more impactful. For example, "I am happy" or "My life is full of love."

Write what you want in life with deeply positive and inspiring feelings. The more you write and repeat these affirmations, the stronger these feelings will grow. Personalize existing affirmations to make them your own and write them down.

 Exercise

> Note the negative thoughts and emotions you wish to change and create affirmations for each of them.

How to write affirmations

People have experimented with various methods to harness the power of written affirmations. Let us explore them.

1. Write with concentration

It is crucial for both your hands and mind to be focused while writing affirmations. If your thoughts wander, you may not achieve the desired outcome. Before starting, you may close your eyes and direct your mind to stay focused throughout the activity. As you write, deeply understand the meaning behind each word. The more you immerse yourself in the task, the greater the likelihood of attracting positivity into your life.

2. Write with positive feelings

When you write with positive feelings, its impact reaches deep into your subconscious mind, accelerating the manifestation of your affirmations. For example, as you write, "I am full of confidence; I succeed in all aspects of life," feel the confidence grow within you. This might take some time initially but use your imagination to help you. Recall past incidents where you acted confidently or visualize how you will embody this quality in the future. This will inspire positive feelings that deeply influence your subconscious mind.

3. Write consistently

You would have likely heard the phrase, "You are the architect of your life." Writing affirmations is a powerful way to experience this firsthand. When you repeatedly write what you aspire to with positive feelings, your subconscious mind accepts it as the truth and attracts evidence into your life. Writing an affirmation consistently for at least 21 days is known to ingrain it in your subconscious and manifest it in your life. Changes may take time but keep up the writing practice without giving up.

4. Sing it while you write it

Read each word aloud. Choose an affirmation, write it in your journal, and read it aloud repeatedly. You can even add a musical tune and hum it. Let it fill your mind throughout the day.

5. Experiment

Try a new method for writing your affirmations daily to keep the activity engaging. If you write in a journal one day, switch to sticky notes or use a whiteboard the next day. Experiment with writing upside down or with your non-dominant hand. Some days, use colorful markers or type your affirmations on your smartphone.

You can also write positive phrases or words like "I am happy" or "I am successful" in places you frequently see, such as your water bottle, mirror, chair, or laptop. Use a permanent marker to write these affirmations on your daily medication box or bottle, turning it into a dose of positive energy.

6. Assess your progress

As you consistently write your affirmations, pay attention to the gradual shifts in your thoughts and feelings. You can celebrate your small successes with rewards and maintain your writing practice with renewed enthusiasm.

When positive affirmations are written consistently with conviction, they soon materialize in your life, often bringing about miraculous results you may never have imagined.

When to write affirmations

An average person has tens of thousands of thoughts daily. The mind moves from one thought to the other, and before you know it, a third thought intrudes, creating an endless chain. If most of these thoughts are negative, you attract and experience sorrow, challenges, and chaos in life. Conversely, if positive thoughts fill your mind more often, you witness transformative changes around you.

A simple way to initiate internal change is by using positive words in your affirmations. For example, instead of writing, "I never make bad financial decisions," write, "I always make well-researched and gainful financial decisions." The vibrations of these positive words influence your thoughts and feelings, steering your life in a new direction.

While this does not mean all challenges will vanish, your approach to solving them will change. As you consistently write and repeat affirmations, every situation will begin to appear like a valuable lesson.

Setting aside time each day for writing affirmations can help you stay consistent. Dedicating 5 to 10 minutes daily is easy, especially for someone as determined as you.

Let us explore two experiments to inspire positive changes in your life.

Experiment 1 – The 3-6-9 method

This experiment involves correlating your goals and affirmations with the numbers 3, 6, and 9. The steps are simple:

- Start by writing your goal or affirmation three times in the morning, when your mind is less cluttered and more receptive. This strengthens the impact of affirmations. Writing your goals thrice is often enough to harness this effect.

- In the afternoon, after lunch, awaken your mind by repeating your goals six times.

- Lastly, write your affirmations nine times before you sleep. Your mind is often crowded at night with thoughts about the day's events. More repetitions of your affirmations will help align you with positive feelings.

- This exercise links your goals and affirmations to patterned numbers, making it easier to remember. Some people may prefer increasing the repetitions, such as using a 4-8-12 or 5-10-15 progression. Whatever pattern you choose, approach the repetitions with understanding, not out of fear or superstition.

Experiment 2 – The 5-55 method

In this experiment, write your goal or affirmation 55 times daily for the next 5 days. Choose a time when you are aligned with your subconscious mind and receptive.

- Begin with small goals. For example, if buying a new smartphone has been on your mind, write, "Thank you, Universe! I have bought my new smartphone, and I am delighted."

- On the fifth day after writing your goal 55 times, feel confident that you have communicated your desire to the Universe. After this, let go of any worry. Focus on your work and trust that your goal will be achieved.

Many neurological studies show that positive self-talk reduces stress, increases efficiency, and enhances the quality of life. It will help you accept situations more readily and adapt to changes more effectively. The key element of the exercise is to connect with your goal at the level of your feelings while writing it. Your feelings and intentions make all the difference.

Exercise

1. Perform the 3-6-9 and 5-55 experiments.

2. Every day, write down any of the following affirmations in your journal 21 times and repeat it:

- I am getting better in every way every day.
- There is an abundance of everything for everyone.
- Whatever I decide to do is indeed possible.
- I am experiencing immense joy, enthusiasm, success, and progress every day.
- I can safely and easily express my feelings.
- I am an outstanding divine creation of God, so my success is assured.

You can even craft your own affirmations and write them down

[9] - To know more, read the book *Inner Magic - The Power of Self-Talk* by Sirshree.

Scan this QR code to order your copy.

26

Goal Setting and Visualization

A dream written down with a date becomes a goal. A goal broken down into steps becomes a plan. A plan backed by action fulfills your dream.

~ Greg Reid

With the arrival of each New Year, many people decide on some goal, from small targets to ambitious dreams. While some diligently strive to achieve their goals, most drift away from their resolutions within a month. Why does this happen?

The primary reason for this lack of commitment is that people set their goals impulsively or due to peer pressure. They think about their goals but don't share them or write them down. Deep down, they know it is a momentary passion destined to fade.

However, some people approach the process with meticulous thought. They carefully examine every aspect, set their goal, write it down, evaluate it thoroughly, analyze its facets, and integrate it into their daily lives.

Achieving significant goals is much like scaling a mountain. To climb a mountain, one must first practice walking and start with small hills, navigating the ups and downs along the way. Maintaining physical health through exercise and a balanced diet is essential. Setting a suitable time according to the weather and making thorough preparations are also crucial steps.

Similarly, to achieve any goal, it is essential to write it down. Writing what you exactly want to experience in life increases the likelihood of its manifestation. Even if you need to adjust your goal over time, you will be physically and mentally prepared for it in advance. Moreover, when you write your goal clearly, you signal to Nature that you are committed and determined to attain it despite any circumstances. Then, Nature also rallies behind you.

Understand how to write down your goal effectively. Write your goal in large letters and place it where you can clearly see it frequently. Ensure your eyes naturally fall on it when you wake up and also during the day, keeping it constantly in mind.

For any goal you set, create a detailed action plan. Regularly reflect on this plan, perhaps weekly or fortnightly, and reassess your strategies. This ongoing review keeps you prepared for upcoming changes or challenges.

Carefully consider each step related to your goal. If you need someone's assistance, inform them well in advance. This proactive approach ensures smooth collaboration and avoids potential setbacks.

Never underestimate your goals. Approach your work daily with unwavering determination, complete surrender, and faith in the supreme power. When you decide your goal, write it down, and resolve to achieve it.

No task is insurmountable. As the saying goes, "Take the first step, and Nature will support you with the rest." Though that initial step may be challenging, writing your goal activates your subconscious mind and rallies the forces of the Universe to aid in its completion.

Therefore, decide your goal today. If you have not decided on your goal yet, make it your goal to decide on your goal soon. Write it down in your journal to solidify your commitment.

 Exercise

    1. Write down your goal

    2. Write down the baby steps to accomplish your goal

    3. Write down the major steps to accomplish your goal

Write from the future to your present self

Once you have meticulously outlined your goals, it is time to shift your perspective. Instead of focusing solely on the journey ahead, imagine you have already arrived at your destination. This practice involves writing a letter as your future self, expressing gratitude to your present self for achieving your goals.

This practice harnesses the power of positive visualization to accelerate your progress toward your goal. By doing so, you are not just dreaming; you are programming your mind for success. This method can significantly boost your motivation, reduce stress, and increase your well-being.

Everyone dreams of a happy and bright future. Regardless of their circumstances, they wish for a better tomorrow and a life filled with happiness, health, and prosperity. They hope to be liked by everyone and respected in society. You, too, would have dreamed about your future. Use your imagination to visualize how your dream will come to fruition.

Imagine you are a teacher or your own profession. You have been placed in a time machine that takes you seven years into the future. Imagine yourself at that time: you have become a college principal. Many students adore you and hold you in high regard. You have earned a doctorate, and your office has a nameplate with your name prefixed with "Dr." You participate in board meetings with high-ranking officers, and you can easily shoulder all the responsibilities that come with your position. You have a large bungalow surrounded by a beautiful garden and have two cars. Your children are now grown and studying in college. Your personality has become more refined. Your hair is turning slightly gray, indicating maturity. You constantly wear a smile, reflecting that you have achieved everything you desired in life. You appear completely content, self-sufficient, calm, and happy.

How does this imagination make you feel? Obviously, you must be thrilled by this imagination!

Now, you need to write down this imagination and the feelings you are experiencing in a letter. You need to write this letter to yourself. Yes, you read that right! You will go seven years into the future, imagine the future you want, and write a letter from the future self to your present self, describing this imagination and the associated feelings. Let us understand how to write this letter.

You may have written letters to someone at some point, or if not, you would have learned letter-writing in school. Keep the letter concise and simple so you can easily read it later. Write the main message in the beginning so that it is not overlooked. Write neatly and legibly. Most importantly, write about your own life instead of discussing changes in the world.

Before writing the letter, reflect on how you attained your current position and achieved what you have today—a good job, a nice home, a comfortable car, etc. For instance, you would have dreamt of buying a house a few years ago. At that time, you might have faced many challenges. But, looking back now, that period may not seem as painful, although you remember the hardships you endured. Today, you feel comfortable, peaceful, and satisfied living in your home. Similarly, you will look at today's dreams and challenges in retrospect after seven years; write about how you will see them from that future perspective.

Express your gratitude for the support system that helped you over the years and led you to today's growth and maturity. Thank your present self for working hard to develop higher virtues.

Here is a sample letter format. Write your name in the blank space and then read it. This will clarify how to write the letter.

> Dear (write your name here),
> Today is the happiest day of my life. My business has reached new heights. It was my dream to build a clothing brand for people of all ages that can cater to everyone's choice in a family, where people find their favorite clothes in one place, with good quality, and within their budget, and see how the dream has come true! My family is proud of me for working hard to realize my dream. I have also managed my health and mastered the art of time management. I am thankful I could work within to inculcate higher qualities like patience, empathy, courage, focus, resilience,

forgiveness, and discipline. I am able to balance between my personal life, family life, and my business smoothly.

My children have received everything they wanted—higher education, a good career, and comfort. They have also embraced values like service to others and putting others first. My hard work has truly paid off.

Although life has taught me a lot slowly and step by step, I am infinitely grateful to my body, mind, intellect, and God for guiding me at every step. I am deeply thankful for every joy, every moment.

Yours,

New (write your name here)

 Exercise

>   Write a letter to yourself visualizing the future you would have achieved. Envision your future with complete faith as if you have already achieved it today. Experience the joy, gratitude, and satisfaction you would feel after achieving everything, and write being immersed in those feelings.

27

Scripting the Blueprint of Your Life

*Writing is an extension of thoughts and feelings,
transcending the limits of time and space.*

When constructing a new house, building, or bridge, a blueprint is created first. A blueprint simplifies overseeing every component, ensuring the plan is thoroughly validated. If interruptions or challenges arise, the blueprint helps identify and resolve issues by revisiting and suitably adjusting the plan.

Similarly, to achieve a goal, you must create a blueprint—a detailed plan written on paper. Outline what you want, how you want it, the possibilities involved, and how to handle any anticipated obstacles. By documenting every detail, your subconscious mind focuses on the goal and works to achieve it in every possible way.

You might wonder, "Can I attract whatever I desire? Is there a simple and effective way to fulfill my dreams?"

Absolutely! When you focus on your goals, feel the joy of achieving them, and write them in your Faith Fair Book with complete faith, the likelihood of them becoming a reality increases.

What is the Faith Fair Book? How do you create one and write your desires in it? Let us explore this.

Some people keep diaries to track their daily expenses, jot down daily sweet and sour experiences, or make to-do lists for the next day. Others use diaries to record personal thoughts, reflections, and ideas.

Today, you will discover a special kind of diary, a powerful tool – the Faith Fair Book. You will write your desires and aspirations with complete faith in your Faith Fair Book, believing they will come true. Use this diary to record everything you wish and hope to achieve in your life.

When you clearly define your goals in all areas of life—the physical, mental, social, financial, and spiritual—in your Faith Fair Book, you are not just expressing your desires but also clarifying your intentions, sending a clear signal to Nature that you have prayed and are awaiting the results. This also helps avoid any unintentional contradictions in your prayers.

People often unintentionally send mixed signals to Nature. For instance, a person might wish for a famous celebrity to visit him, then decide it would be better if they didn't visit, and later hope for a distant relative to visit instead. When all these conflicting wishes are unclear, they might end up in a chaotic situation where everyone shows up at once. This happens because Nature did not receive a clear signal about what was truly desired. The person might think, "But I never wanted this." Indeed, he did not want this exactly, but he was unclear about what he really wanted. To avoid such confusion, clearly write down what you exactly want in your Faith Fair Book.

Some might question how writing down desires can actually make them come true. They may see it as mere theory and doubt whether things can really change just by putting their wishes on paper.

Instead of mindlessly wishing for things like a daydreamer who builds castles in the air, it is important to think about how you will handle the results of your desires. Reflect on how you will manage the outcomes if your wishes come true. Are you prepared for any unexpected consequences? When writing down your desires, consider how their fulfillment will impact your life.

Impulsive desires, without proper thought, can lead to unexpected and undesirable results, as seen in the earlier example. Therefore, take time to reflect on what you truly want. Consider what you want to see, hear, eat, the kind of life you wish to live, the company you seek, and the type of people you want around you, etc.

You should write your desires in the Faith Fair Book only after careful contemplation. Trust that whatever you write in this book is significant and will impact the direction and condition of your life. By writing with faith and a clear vision of your desired outcome, you can bring about the meaningful changes you have long desired.

How to write a Faith Fair Book

Consider the following things when writing a Faith Fair Book:

1. Avoid using the word "no"

Everyone wishes for good, positive things and even prays for them, yet they still face many challenges. For example, someone might pray, "O God, please safeguard me and my family from calamities. May no one fall sick or suffer. Bless us with happiness and protect us from pain, sorrow, and difficulties. Although the prayer seems apt at first glance, it unknowingly contains negative wording.

When you say, "I don't want this. I don't want that," the subconscious mind does not understand the "no" word and instead attracts the very thing it is trying to avoid. As a result, suffering, illness, pain, sorrow, and problems follow in your life.

Let us try a quick experiment: Close your eyes and think, "I don't want to see a pink elephant."

What did you see? A pink elephant, right? This happens because the subconscious does not process the concept of "not pink." It can only recognize the image of an elephant, so it creates one in your mind regardless of its pink or black color. As a result, you visualized a pink elephant, even though no such elephant exists in reality. Therefore, instead of focusing on what you don't want, always clearly state what you really want.

2. Write completely

Write down your thoughts, desires, and goals clearly and completely. You may often speak or write things partialy, assuming the other person will understand its full meaning. But the other person might not necessarily interpret things as you do. You might know the complete context, but the other person may not. Therefore, always articulate what you want in clear, precise words, including the reason behind it, so that Nature receives a clear signal as to why you want to fulfill your desire or goal.

Keep in mind that Nature is eagerly waiting for your clear communication to manifest your desired outcome. The more specific and comprehensive your description, the better equipped Nature will be to respond to your requests.

3. Write in the present tense

When writing down your goals or desires, use the present tense instead of the past or future tense. Write as if the outcomes are happening right now or have already happened.

For example, you want to secure a good job where you work in synergy with your team, receive appreciation for your work, earn a substantial salary, and impress your subordinates and seniors. You might write: "I work in a Fortune 500 company where I collaborate effectively with my team, supporting each other to achieve outstanding results. My colleagues respect me and regularly commend my contributions. The company values my work and compensates me generously, enabling me to meet all my needs and those of my family comfortably."

4. Set a time frame

Begin writing the diary with the desires you want to fulfill within the first year. Clearly specify each desire and the timeline for achieving it.

Just as you used to draft a rough book first and then transfer it to the fair book during school days, follow the same process in writing the Faith Fair Book.

First, write your initial ideas, desires, and goals in a rough book. Then, after careful consideration, write them down in the Faith Fair Book using clear and refined words.

For instance, if you want to lose weight, you might write: "One year from today, I want to be lighter by 10 kg. My weight will be 60 kg at that time, which is my ideal weight. It has happened. I look beautiful in a well-fitting dress. This ideal weight has made my body more agile, allowing me to perform all activities easily."

5. Create or attach pictures

If you are more visually oriented than auditory, you can draw images or cut and paste relevant pictures from newspapers or magazines into your Faith Fair Book instead of writing. Regularly revisit these pictures in your Faith Fair Book to boost your enthusiasm.

In addition, you can use a manifestation board or vision board. To create this, first write down your goals, dreams, and aspirations. Then, gather related images from magazines or prints from the internet. Paste them onto a thick cardboard sheet or poster board. If you wish, you may write some inspirational quotes or thoughts with colored pens to motivate yourself.

Place your vision board where you will see it often. This constant visual reminder will keep you motivated and focused on achieving your goals.

Suffixing "...so that..."

Often, you might desire to achieve something without being clear about why you really want it. Sometimes, you might pursue things simply because you see others doing or having them, which can lead to regret later. Therefore, when you write down a desire, clarify its reason.

For instance, when a child asks their parents for money, the parents often ask them questions like, "Why do you need it?" or "What will you do with it?" If the child clearly explains why they need the money, the parents are more likely to agree and fulfill their request. Similarly, when you ask Nature for something, you must explain the reason clearly.

Therefore, whatever you want to see happening in your life, write it in your Faith Fair Book by appending the phrase "...so that..." to clarify your reasons. This phrase will prompt you to write new sentences that provide a clear explanation to Nature.

For example, if you write "I want a car" in your diary, write with faith why you want it by adding "so that" in your sentences. Write, "I want a car so that I can use my valuable time effectively… so that I can travel with ease and safety in all seasons… so that I can visit places and enjoy the beauty of Nature… so that I can enjoy traveling with my family in complete health and happiness… so that I get the opportunity to express my qualities…" and so on.

You can use "…so that…" not only for material things but also when writing prayers to overcome your habits and patterns.

For example, if you want to practice yoga, you can write: "I want to practice yoga every day so that my digestion improves, my mind and body become purer and healthier, and I can complete all my tasks efficiently with renewed energy."

If you want to wake up early but struggle due to laziness, it is time to give Nature a clear signal. Write in your diary: "I want to wake up early in the morning so that I can enjoy the fresh morning air… so that I can feel enthusiastic and revitalized throughout the day… so that I can start my day with meditation to keep my mind energized."

In this way, adding "…so that…" will enhance the power of your prayer. You can even add "…so that…" to negative sentences to turn them into positive ones. However, do this only when you cannot frame a positive sentence.

For example, if you write, "I don't want to face any problems or accidents during my journey," add, "…so that my journey is pleasant and comfortable …so that I can enjoy reaching my destination on time."

Writing your Faith Fair Book this way will make it more effective and meaningful and deepen your alignment with Nature. After expressing your thoughts positively and clearly, you will experience inner peace and also start living life free from entanglements. You can ask for whatever you want in life from the bottom of your heart as you build a strong conviction that Nature has abundant resources for everyone and grants them according to their desires.

 Exercise

1. Write about your desired state of health.
2. Write about the qualities you want to see in yourself.
3. Write about your financial goals.
4. Write about your relationship goals.

Empower your writing with feelings

People often manifest many positive things in their lives, but without knowing how to handle them, they fall into addictions and bad habits. To prevent this, it is crucial to give clear instructions to Nature so that it understands and manifests your wishes. For example, someone might win a lottery but, due to ignorance, develop habits like alcoholism and gambling. This happens because they did not clarify why they wanted, what they wanted. So, let us understand how to convey your message to Nature clearly.

1. Whatever you believe in becomes the truth of your life and manifests in your world. Whether it is prosperity or poverty, health or illness, happiness or sadness, good or bad, respect or disrespect—everything appears in your life according to your beliefs.

As the name suggests, the Faith Fair Book is the Fair Book of Faith, where you write mindfully with full faith and patience. Whatever you write in this book signifies that you are conveying it directly to Nature, God. This is a simple, pure prayer arising from the heart.

Therefore, you can start writing with a small prayer. A short prayer is given below. If you wish, you may repeat it or rewrite it in your own words.

"O God, I am about to write all my desires. I know you will grant me only what I am eligible and worthy of. Please help me raise my understanding, eligibility, and worthiness."

2. The outcome of what you write always manifests depending on the feeling with which you write. Always write from a sense of havingness—feeling that what you want is already given and manifested and let go of any feelings of lack.

   For example, you might desire a car, a luxurious house, money, or harmonious relationships. However, even after writing positive things, your mind could be filled with doubts like, "How is this possible? I can never get this. I am not destined to receive this. The car or luxurious house is farfetched; I don't have my own house. My family members will never change; they keep quarreling."

   With such doubts, you are placing your feet in two different boats. This makes manifesting your desires an uphill battle. With such pendulum-like swinging of feelings, things you were meant to receive from Nature either stop midway or take time to manifest. Therefore, always write with a singular feeling of havingness, "I am so happy that I have already received this."

   A person once asked his Guru, "O Master, there is a railway crossing on my way to the office, and the gate is always closed when I get there. Whether I leave home ten minutes early or late, I always find the gate closed." The Guru responded, "Give up the thought that you always find the gate closed. Instead, repeat, 'I always find that gate open. I reach the office on time. I use my time properly and work without stress." When he changed his mindset, he began to find the gate open. This is the power of living in the feeling of havingness.

   So, whenever you experience something negative in life, see it as an opportunity to give a clear signal to Nature. Do not view negative things as bad; instead, say, "This is giving me an indication, an opportunity to write the right prayer."

3. It is very important to align your words and feelings while writing. For example, Vijay wrote in his Faith Fair Book, "I want to go on a leisure trip to Dubai with my family and enjoy my vacation." However, while writing, his thoughts were filled with concern, "Planning for so many people will be complicated. The expenses will be high. I'll need to take

everyone's preferences to avoid complaints." His words expressed a wish, but his feelings were dominated by worry. This misalignment can hinder the fulfillment of the desire or make the experience less enjoyable than expected.

Therefore, as you write, cultivate the feeling of happiness. Recall an experience when your wish was fulfilled, and you felt overjoyed. By reliving that pleasant memory, you transport yourself to a state of havingness, invoking those joyous feelings once again. This positive feeling will infuse your writing with enthusiasm.

The ultimate use of the Faith Fair Book

The Faith Fair Book is not merely a tool for accumulating wealth or fulfilling mundane desires. It can be a powerful instrument for spiritual growth and realizing your higher purpose. Instead of focusing solely on material possessions, you should use your Faith Fair Book to manifest a meaningful life by connecting with the Source within and unlocking its fullest potential.

Once you shift from a negative mindset plagued by limiting beliefs to the positive feeling of havingness, you need to use the Faith Fair Book as a catapult to transform your life and lead to transcendence, where you realize your true nature and manifest its divine qualities.

By setting intentions aligned with divine qualities, you can contribute to the greater good. Imagine using your Faith Fair Book to manifest compassion, kindness, and wisdom in your daily interactions and positively impact the world around you.

When you focus on manifesting your higher purpose, you tap into the Source of Creation. You attract opportunities that align with your divine plan and allow you to fulfill your ultimate life purpose. Instead of chasing fleeting pleasures, you can create a lasting legacy that benefits not only you but also those around you.

28

Gratitude and Admiration

*Be thankful for what you have; you'll end up having more.
If you concentrate on what you don't have,
you will never ever have enough.*

~ Oprah Winfrey

Two very close childhood friends, Ajay and Suresh, reunited after many years and eagerly wanted to spend some quality time together. To make the most of their reunion, they planned a fun-filled trip to Goa for four to five days. The train journey was a delight as they chatted, shared their experiences, and admired the beautiful scenery.

Having grown up in different environments, their habits, hobbies, and lifestyles were quite different. On the first day, everything seemed perfect. However, on the second day, Ajay slept late as he was not accustomed to waking up early. Meanwhile, Suresh, who enjoyed early morning walks, went for a stroll. When Suresh returned, he saw Ajay still sleeping soundly. He tried to wake him up, but Ajay slept like a log. Slightly annoyed, Suresh decided to go for breakfast alone.

When Suresh finished breakfast and returned, Ajay was still in bed. Frustrated, Suresh called out, "Get up, Ajay! How much do you plan to sleep? Why did we even come here if you wanted to sleep all day?" Hearing this, Ajay woke up and silently went for a shower, angry but choosing to stay calm. That day, they explored the landmark churches in Goa. The next day, they planned to visit the beach early in the morning.

But just like the previous day, Ajay did not wake up on time despite their plan. Suresh was enraged. He went to the beach alone, lost in negative thoughts about Ajay. He started remembering small things from childhood, like how Ajay was late for school and never cared about time. Engrossed in these thoughts, he picked up a stick and wrote in the sand, "Today, I am very angry with Ajay's careless behavior." He did not notice that Ajay had arrived and was reading what he wrote in the sand but chose to stay silent. Suresh felt better after writing it down on the sand, and they started talking. The rest of the day went well.

On the third day, Ajay woke up early, and both got ready to visit a fort on a hill. While climbing, Ajay climbed a bit ahead. The path was slippery, and suddenly Suresh slipped and fell. He called out to Ajay loudly, unable to get up due to a twisted leg. Ajay quickly ran to him, helped him up, and made him sit on a large rock nearby. Ajay said, "Don't worry, I will call for help, and we will visit a doctor." He left and returned with someone to assist them. He noticed that Suresh had etched on the rock, "Today, Ajay has helped me a lot. I am so grateful to him. Thank you, Ajay!"

Without saying a word, Ajay and the helper supported Suresh and took him to the doctor. After the treatment, they returned to the hotel, where Suresh had his prescribed medicine and slept. By evening, his pain had significantly reduced.

The next day, they had to return. While chatting at night, Ajay asked Suresh, "On the second day, you were angry and wrote on the sand. But on the third day, you wrote on the stone. Why?" Suresh replied, "I wrote on the sand when I was angry so the writing would be swept by the waves and fade away. I did not want my anger to last long or be remembered. When you helped me, I wrote it on stone because I wanted to remember it forever."

Hearing this, Ajay felt emotional and shared his feelings as well. They forgave each other and expressed their gratitude, their friendship reaching a new level, helping elevate each other's consciousness.

This story teaches us that whenever we feel hurt by someone's words, get angry, or have negative emotions, we should write them in places like sand, soil, water, or the sky. This means writing them where they can naturally fade away. This way, those feelings do not linger and disappear like the wind or waves.

However, some things you want to remember for your entire life, such as gratitude, appreciation, help, and support, should be written on something permanent, like stone. This means writing them in your diary, smartphone, or laptop so that they remain with you for a lifetime.

It is often seen that someone helps us during the day. We say thanks for significant help and remember it, but do we pay attention to the small acts of kindness? We often do not remember those because we do not give them importance or consider them as help.

For instance, suppose you see a long ticket queue and ask the person in front to get your ticket. After receiving the ticket, you thank them mechanically and move on. By evening, you might forget the incident. But now, perform a new task of jotting down the essence of that small act of kindness.

Similarly, observe the help you receive throughout the day. For example, if you do not have change, and the cab driver or shopkeeper lets you go without taking the change; you went to a shop to buy something the shopkeeper didn't have, but he procured it from elsewhere for you; you went on vacation, and your neighbor watered your plants; someone offered you a seat on a bus or train; someone held the elevator door for you; someone helped you park your car.

Though such incidents are common and often go unnoticed, let alone writing about them, you may have said thank you for these small acts but did not feel gratitude deeply. You might not feel it during the incident and let it go as a trivial thing without much thought. However, while writing, when you recall many such incidents, you will realize that so many people helped you throughout the day, making your tasks easier and saving time and energy. Then, you will start feeling gratitude and love.

Just as small beads form a necklace or bricks and cement form a house, expressing gratitude for these little things will bring significant changes and attract more positivity.

Create a gratitude journal

We have been provided with family and relationships to enrich and beautify our lives. We form deep connections within these relationships.

Everyone in a family does much for each other and also holds expectations. However, over time, we may start living mechanically and take each other for granted. Despite receiving so much from our family, many of us often fail to express gratitude. This is because we hesitate to say "Thank you" to our family members, having never learned to do so since childhood. No one taught us, nor did we see or hear others doing it.

Additionally, Nature provides abundant air, water, and food. Many animals, microbes, and plants contribute to our well-being: dogs guard our homes, honeybees provide honey, and cattle give us milk. Yet, we seldom thank them. Even though our bodies function tirelessly to fulfill our wishes day and night, they rarely receive our gratitude. We were rarely taught to express gratitude for all this. We might internally know and believe that the whole universe is helping us, but we do not understand how important it is to express gratitude verbally.

Therefore, create a gratitude journal today where you write thanks to everyone and everything. When we express our gratitude in writing, the likelihood of expressing it verbally increases. Until we start verbalizing our gratitude, at least we should express it in writing. By verbalizing and writing thanks, we convey to Nature that we are filled with love and gratitude for everyone and everything that cares for us. Consequently, what we express gratitude for, grows in our life.

Here are some examples of what to write in your gratitude journal:

- First and foremost, I thank God, Ishwar, Allah, the Almighty, the higher power for sending me to Earth in the human form.
- I am thankful to Nature, whose five elements have created and continue to sustain this body.
- I thank this body for helping me experience my aliveness and allowing me to enjoy all the experiences of the physical world.
- I am thankful to my parents for giving birth to me.
- I am thankful to all my relatives and friends who have supported me at every step of my life. (You can thank all your relatives, friends, teachers, neighbors, colleagues, helpers, pets, birds, and plants.)

- I am thankful to my home for protecting me in all seasons and making me feel safe and comfortable.

- I am thankful to my room and bed for giving me a good night's sleep and refreshing me. (Also, thank your mobile phone, laptop, car, bike, watch, and everything in your room.)

- I am thankful to my maid, milkman, gardener, driver, grocer, and others for helping me live comfortably.

- I am thankful to all the incidents in my life for helping me understand higher values and grow in life.

Most importantly, thank every part of your body for contributing to the functioning of the whole body. When you write about gratitude, you begin to feel it. This practice helps you become a better human being. A gratitude journal makes you more aware; you start paying attention to what you are thankful for instead of taking it for granted.

Every day, whenever you have time, write at least three sentences of gratitude for three new things in your journal. By continuously writing gratitude in this way, gradually, it will become easier for you to express gratitude in words, bringing you peace and contentment.

 Exercise

Write down your gratitude for the ten most important things in your life.

Pen down your admiration

Just as we often hesitate to express gratitude, we also hesitate to praise others. Despite our desire, we stop ourselves by thinking, "What might the other person think of me?" However, when you genuinely admire someone from your heart with joy, they will feel good about it. Moreover, they may focus more on their qualities and strive to enrich them further.

Some of these people may be your acquaintances, while others may be strangers you encounter along the way. Appreciate their qualities in your journal. This practice will also benefit you because when you honor the qualities in others, those qualities begin to manifest within you. If you already possess those qualities, they multiply because Nature perceives your appreciation and finds ways to enhance them in your life.

This also means that if you want to nurture a quality in yourself, proactively seek out someone who already possesses it and write down a few words of praise for them. Even if you cannot directly express it to them today, by repeatedly writing it down, a desire will awaken within you to convey it to them, and soon you will do so with ease. Start by writing praises for the qualities of your friends or family members.

Let us see how you can write praise or admiration for someone's qualities:

If you have observed someone speaking lovingly, write: "I am very impressed by this person's (write the name if known or write a reference to the situation where you noticed the quality) friendly and affectionate behavior."

Vivek loved his family, especially his mom. He noticed how she spent her entire day in the kitchen, cooking everyone's favorite meal, neatly organizing their belongings, and preparing his father's things for work. She went to bed after everyone else and woke up before anyone else to keep things ready. Despite all her efforts, no one thanked or appreciated her. Vivek loved his mother dearly but kept silent and hesitated to thank and appreciate her. He struggled to appreciate anyone even though he wanted to.

One day, Vivek bought a diary with the message: "You are praiseworthy for whatever you write." This simple sentence inspired him. He realized he could use the diary to write down his appreciation for those he found hard to praise in person or for those he felt deserved recognition, but his mind kept saying, "It's their duty anyway. What's there to appreciate for that?"

From that day on, he dedicated 10 minutes every day to writing about his admiration of the qualities of people whom he could not appreciate in person. He began with his family, commending every small or big task they did. As he did this, he felt a more profound sense of love for them. Gradually, he started praising everyone for every little thing he liked about them.

If you face a similar challenge, start at home; it is your practice ground. You might be surprised at the miracles a simple word of gratitude can bring. Whether you seek positive energy, direction, joy, success, or prosperity, begin by writing these desires down and saying them aloud. Also, admire and acknowledge those who embody these qualities.

Similarly, take pleasure in the beauty of Nature around you—relish the rainy season, gaze at the moon and stars, and enjoy the chirping of birds. Write praises for these marvels. Nature is full of wonders. Every morning, the rising sun spreads its light everywhere. The weather knows when it is time to change without being told. Creatures of all kinds, whether on land or in water, receive their share of food. Life evolves with time. From a single seed, thousands of flowers and fruits bloom. These are all miracles to marvel at!

Have you ever taken a moment to appreciate Nature's wonders and express gratitude? Write down all these marvels in your journal today and watch positive changes unfold in your life.

Here are some examples of how you could write in your journal:

- The sun's glowing rays are infusing everyone's life with rejuvenating energy.
- The steady flow of the river signifies that my life is flowing in the right direction.
- Flowers spread their fragrance, sharing joy and contentment with everyone.

As you begin to praise and thank people, things, and Nature, the qualities within you will flourish even more.

 Exercise

1. Write your admiration for Nature.
2. Write your admiration for your family.
3. Write your admiration for your friends and colleagues.
4. Write the following affirmation 21 times and repeat it: "There is an abundance of everything for everyone."

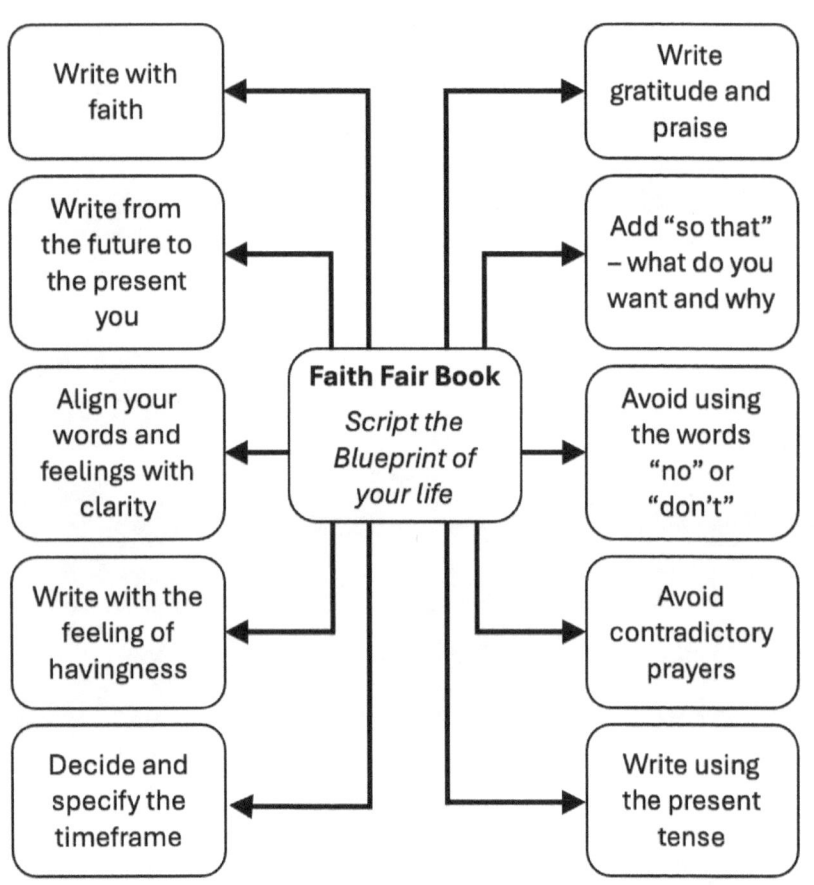

PART 6

TRANSCENDENTAL WRITING

29

Connecting with the Source

Your intuition knows what to write, so get out of the way.
~ Ray Bradbury

When your mind is cluttered with doubts and uncertainties and unsure what to do next, put your thoughts on paper. Write down your problems and concerns. As you continue writing, the fog will lift, and clarity will emerge. It is like watching the sun break through the clouds. Soon, you will discover solutions you had not considered before. When you let go of thoughts and surrender the problem to Nature, Nature begins to work for you.

This is the Seventh Law of Writing, which states that writing empties the mind, allowing the inner wise voice of the Source to express itself.

Following are some ways of connecting with the Source and seeking guidance.

Quota Technique

When the mind is caught up in a dilemma, multiple thoughts arise simultaneously. The mind resists writing and makes excuses to avoid writing. At such times, you can use the Quota technique.

In the quota technique, first write down numbers from 1 to 10. Then, write down ten thoughts related to your problem or dilemma. For example, if you have a financial issue, first write down each thought that comes to your mind, one by one, from 1 to 10. As you write, you will find that most of your thoughts have subsided, making you feel slightly calmer if not completely relieved.

However, if you find more thoughts after writing from 1 to 10, increase the number from 11 to 20 and jot down your thoughts. You will see that all your thoughts about the financial problem are exhausted, effectively emptying you of thoughts.

At this time, sit quietly for a few moments. This is a waiting time; pause and allow yourself to connect with the Source within. Connecting with the Source implies being in the feeling of aliveness that exists regardless of thoughts, where only peace prevails. Now, new thoughts may arise that have never occurred before. Start writing them down as they emerge, whether related to the problem or altogether different. As you keep writing, you will align with the Source and allow it to write through you. Keep writing as long as the urge to write persists. After you stop writing, read what you have written. You will likely find a solution to your dilemma or a related hint.

Remember, when you write down your emotions and thoughts honestly and sincerely, the accumulated grime of years begins to melt away from the mind, your subconscious mind is emptied of past impressions. You start receiving guidance from the Source within. Therefore, whenever you feel distressed, sit in silence to connect with the Source and receive solutions to problems[10].

Grasping Nature's hints

Nature often gives us hints and ideas to solve our problems, but we are so caught up in our thoughts that we fail to notice these hints. However, putting our thoughts on paper effectively empties the mind. An empty mind allows us to focus on new things and grasp the cues from Nature.

When some people are faced with a problem and cannot find a solution, they open a random page of a holy scripture and read a verse or a line. They firmly believe that Nature, God, Ishwar, Allah, whatever you regard as the supreme power, will show the way through that sacred book.

Similarly, to find a way to solve a problem, you can use a dictionary or any random book. First, write your problem in your journal. Then, randomly open a dictionary page and find a word denoting an object. Now, link that object to your problem and contemplate how it could relate to your situation.

For example, suppose you are facing a relationship problem, and the word you come across is "fan." Now, reflect on how your problem might relate to "fan." Write down all possible ideas in your journal. For instance, a fan has three to four blades that rotate while its central rod remains stable. Similarly, you can have different relationships with everyone, but the core bonding of love is constant. Everyone's thinking could differ, but the family remains united and unbroken. Relationships could have problems; everyone's viewpoints can be distinct, yet the underlying purpose of relationships is worth persevering. By reflecting in this way, you will come up with several ideas. Writing them down gives shape to the right guidance meant for you.

In this way, you can find solutions to your problems with the help of Nature. Whatever the situation in your life, write it down to seek guidance from Nature.

Whenever you write down an incident honestly and express your experiences, emotions, and mental state accurately, you also understand what Nature wants to teach you through the incident. When you thoroughly reflect on it by writing it down, you begin to recognize Nature's cues. Nature brings events into your life to help you learn your life lessons thoroughly.

 Exercise

1. Write your problem.

2. Write down a word denoting an object from the dictionary or a book.

3. Relate (1) and (2) and write down your contemplation.

Learn from events in life

No one can claim that their life has been the same throughout. Experiencing events, positive or negative, is an inevitable part of life. Of course, the proportion of positive and negative events in life may vary. Sometimes, negative events can be more frequent, and at times, positive ones. Every event brings with it a gift and teaches us life lessons. However, the human mind tends to focus on the negative aspects of everything. It pays less attention to happiness and more to sorrow.

You might have noticed that when an event happens, the mind keeps comparing and judging it. Even a trivial incident might seem like a mountain at that moment, but after many years, the mind says, "If it were not for that incident, I would have continued to live in the same old way." In other words, every event contributes to our growth, but we understand it later by hindsight.

Whatever your age today, numerous events would have happened in your life that have contributed to your growth. Yet, sometimes, due to a lack of understanding, you might have been entangled in an event that might have negatively impacted your life, aggravating the challenges. But how do you feel when you recall that event after so many years? Does it still affect you as much as it did then, or has it become less intense?

Write down all the events in every area of your life and analyze them according to your present understanding, noting what you learned from them.

1. Financial event

For instance, if you had a financial problem at some point, what was your state then? What kind of thoughts troubled you? What were your emotions? What was your mind saying? Reflect on everything and write down each aspect of that event. Detail the steps you took to resolve that problem and describe what benefits or losses you incurred.

2. Occupational event

When people try to stand up for themselves after a certain age, they may face many challenges. You, too, might have faced some challenges or pressures related to your job or business. Write about an event related to your career. What were the challenges and what actions did you take? What were the outcomes of those actions? What did you learn from your choices?

3. Relational or social event

Human connection is fundamental to our existence, encompassing relationships with loved ones, peers, and community. These interactions weave a rich and diverse tapestry of experiences - uplifting, difficult, surprising, or life-changing. Write about a significant event involving these relationships and how they have shaped the journey of your life. How was your mental and emotional state while going through these myriad experiences? Did your relationships grow stronger or encounter obstacles?

4. Health-related event

Modern life presents universal health challenges affecting people of all ages. Factors like unhealthy eating habits and environment contribute to various health concerns, from minor to major. Even the young are not immune.

Write about a significant health experience from your life. What problems did you face, and what proactive measures do you now take to safeguard your well-being? How did you emotionally navigate the challenge - with resilience or anxiety? Reflect on the lessons learned and your transformed approach to health. Write them all down,

You can write about any other event and contemplate it. What were your thoughts and emotions at the time and later? Were your thoughts more negative or positive? Did you learn a lesson from it, or remain stuck in sorrow? Recall every emotion carefully, write it down, and try to understand it from a new perspective.

 Exercise

    1. Specify an event.

    2. Contemplate and write about it in detail.

    3. Write what you learned from it.

Talk to your ideal

Everyone has faith in someone, be it their parents, God or Nature, a Guru or Teacher, an advisor or well-wisher, a friend, or a trustworthy person. This faith runs so deep that no matter what others say, the person seeks counsel from their trusted ones. The words of these trusted individuals are like words carved in stone.

Does this trust develop on its own, or is there a reason behind it?

The reason is that the people in whom we have faith have a higher level of consciousness and a wealth of knowledge. And most importantly, their vibrations match ours, meaning there is tuning between us and them. It is akin to the companionship of Krishna and Arjuna, the relationship of a guru and disciple.

Whenever someone shares their problem with their trusted ones, they begin to view the event with detachment. As they are not emotionally attached to the event, it becomes easier for them to understand its intricacies. When a problem or event is viewed with detachment, finding a solution becomes easier.

We may have often noticed that we can easily offer a solution when we listen to someone else's problem. But when the same problem occurs to us, we get stuck in it. Then, we need someone else's support. Why does it happen that we can guide others but forget the same guidance when we need it the most? It is because we get stuck in our own problems. As problems overwhelm us with sadness, we are rarely able to see the right solution. Therefore, we feel the need for someone to guide us.

You must also be trusting many people in your life. Among them, there must be at least one person with whom you can open your heart and share everything as if opening up your entire book. Their words seem like divine guidance to you. You try to embrace their advice and apply it to your life. Sometimes, you meet such people around you. Even if you don't, you can still communicate with them by matching their vibrations.

Such communication aims to receive guidance from the Source. However, sometimes, the people we want to seek advice from are away from us, or for some reason, it is not possible to talk to them. But now you can receive their guidance in an imaginary form through writing.

In this method, first, decide from whom you will seek guidance. If there is no such person in your life, you can have an imaginary conversation with God, Ishwar, Allah, the Universe, or whoever you believe in. Then, with a book and pen, start conversing with them. Focus on what the solution to the problem would be according to them. In other words, you should think of the answer from their perspective. In this way, the answers will change when you start thinking from their point of view. Then, the words or thoughts that arise within will be their advice.

Remember, whatever you discuss with them here will be in writing. You need to write down the dialogues of yourself as well as theirs. Your mind might provide the answer initially, but as you continue writing, your mind will calm down, and the answers will emerge from the Source. You will realize that this is the proper guidance.

Let us understand this with an example of a daughter talking to her father and finding a solution to her problem.

Rashi had immense faith in her father. She sought his advice for every problem and wrote down the advice he gave. After her wedding, she had to move to another city, but she continued to share every issue or problem with him. Over time, she became busy tending to her home and children. She did not have much time to talk to her father. So, whenever a problem arose, she would mentally converse with him, write down everything, and get the apt answer.

This time, she was in a dilemma. She wanted to work but did not want to leave her children at home, and there was no pressing need for money. But the children had grown up and could take care of themselves. Her in-laws and house-help could take care of them. She was educated and wanted to focus on her career and do something for herself now. To resolve this dilemma, she sought her father's advice in writing. She sat with a diary and pen.

Rashi: Father, the children have grown up and can manage everything independently. I want to work now to benefit from my degree and fulfill my dream of becoming a professional. I want to achieve something in life, but I am worried about how the children will manage in my absence. I am concerned that my in-laws do not face any trouble. What should I do?

Father: Yes, you are right. In a year or two, the children will start studying in college, and then you will have all the time in the world. If you start now, the timing will be just right. Talk to your in-laws and see what they have to say.

Mind (interjecting in between): But is there a need to work? What is lacking at home? You will only add more running around to your routine. Relax at home, go shopping, and enjoy life.

Rashi: I don't enjoy all of that. How much TV should I watch, and how much shopping can I do? If I am not going anywhere outside, why should I shop? I want to develop myself and fulfill my dreams.

Father: Talk to Akash (Rashi's husband), your in-laws, and your children. See what they say. If they agree, start with a part-time job. Work 2 to 3 hours and devote the rest to the children and home. Try this for a year! This way, you will get some practice.

Rashi: This will be a good solution. No one at home will object, and I will stay engaged in work.

Mind: But can you handle both home and office? Everyone is used to you being around; how will you manage everything?

Rashi: Everything will be fine, don't worry. We have a house-help too, remember? Gradually, everyone will get used to it.

Father: Give it a try. If it seems difficult, there are online jobs you can do from home. Nowadays, you can work from home. If you think about it, you can find ways to do it.

Rashi: Yes, Father! I will talk to everyone at home today and start looking for a job. Your words have given me strength and boosted my courage. I will take the first step and see what happens.

In this way, Rashi had an imaginary written conversation with her father and understood his perspective. She agreed with his advice that initially, she should take up an online part-time job for a year and then extend the duration later. No one would object to this.

You, too, can find solutions to your problems by having imaginary written conversations with your well-wisher, Guru, God, or the Source. When you talk to them, your mind will also interject. If you understand that "This is the mind's chatter; my ideal would not say such things," then you can write separate dialogues for the mind as Rashi did. Also, try to see how they would talk if they were in front of you, talking to you.

Initially, it may take some time to believe that what is being written comes from the Source. But after a while, you will gradually start connecting with the Source. Once you become familiar, you will connect with the Source as soon as you start writing.

 Exercise

Virtually discuss a problem with your ideal in writing using the below format.

You: ………………………………………………………….

Ideal: ………………………………………………………….

Mind: ………………………………………………………….

You: ………………………………………………………….

Ideal: ………………………………………………………….

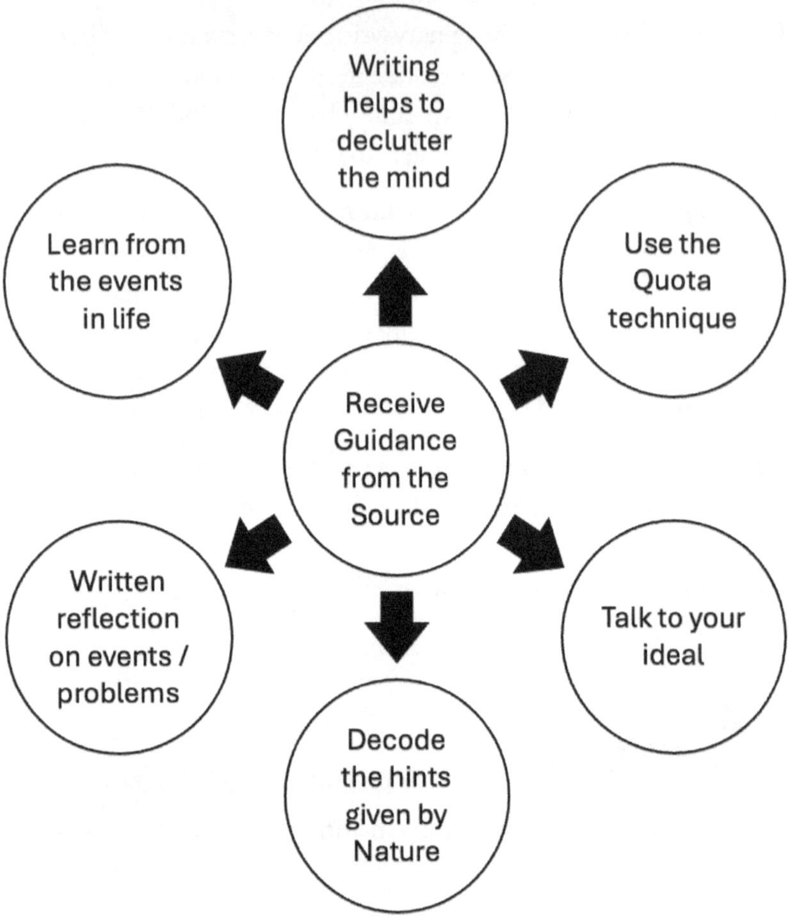

```
                    ┌─────────────┐
                    │   Writing   │
                    │   helps to  │
                    │   declutter │
                    │   the mind  │
                    └─────────────┘
                           ▲
   ┌──────────┐            │            ┌──────────┐
   │ Learn from│           │            │  Use the │
   │ the events│◀──┐       │       ┌───▶│   Quota  │
   │  in life  │   │       │       │    │ technique│
   └──────────┘    │  ┌─────────┐  │    └──────────┘
                   └──│ Receive │──┘
                      │ Guidance│
                   ┌──│from the │──┐
                   │  │ Source  │  │
   ┌──────────┐    │  └─────────┘  │    ┌──────────┐
   │  Written │◀───┘       │       └───▶│ Talk to  │
   │reflection│            │            │ your     │
   │on events/│            ▼            │ ideal    │
   │ problems │    ┌─────────────┐      └──────────┘
   └──────────┘    │   Decode    │
                   │  the hints  │
                   │   given by  │
                   │   Nature    │
                   └─────────────┘
```

 [10] - To know more, read the book T*he Secret of Alignment* by Sirshree.

Scan this QR code to order your copy.

30

Writing from the Source

Fill your paper with the breathings of your heart.
~ William Wordsworth

Ancient scriptures like the Vedas and Upanishads venerate the glory of the Creator, the Source of all creation. The Source is ever present and all-pervading. Every human being holds within oneself the possibility of being instrumental in experiencing and expressing the Source.

The ancient sages and saints who scribed the holy scriptures were in perfect alignment with the Source. They could download the profound truths that emerged from the Source by dwelling in inner silence, thus serving as pens for the Source to write through them.

You can manifest the Creator's plan only when the first creation happens. The first creation is to seek inspiration from the Creator within by accessing inner silence in the background of the mind.

You can see the expression of creativity all around you—be it a painting, a business plan, poetry, a song, or a scientific breakthrough. When you enter the creative process to write, paint, create music, or even allow ideas to emerge, you actually connect with the Source within; you touch the inner silence at your heart.

Creation from the silence of the Source in the heart is novel, intuitive, innovative, and wondrous. On the other hand, creation from the clutter of thoughts in the head is superficial, limited, and a copy of what already exists in the world.

When you connect with the Source in the silence of the heart, immense clarity is experienced. This clarity is effortless and spontaneous. Whatever is expressed from the Source connects with others at a deeper level. It awakens the Source within them.

When one who has never read the Vedas or Upanishads connects with the Source within, what emerges is nothing less than the wisdom of these scriptures. People may wonder how what is being expressed strikingly resembles scriptural wisdom. This happens because whatever is written from the Source is the voice of the Creator.

Saint Kabir composed *dohas*, couplets, Saint Tukaram composed *abhangas*, hymns, Prophet Mohammad scripted the *Holy Quran*. Though none of them had any formal education in spiritual wisdom, their creation resembled the prior scriptures like the Vedas and Upanishads. This indeed is a testimony that the Source expressed its universal truths through them all, as they remained surrendered to the cause of the Source.

In the same way, for original creation to happen through you, you must surrender to the divine will and lend your voice to the Source within rather than the ego.

The faith of God[11]

Faith bridges the gap between thought and manifestation, encouraging us to trust that what is unseen will eventually come to pass. It is a common belief that "seeing is believing," but true faith is about trusting in what is yet to be seen. You place complete trust in divine timing and the slow, deliberate unfolding of life's events in alignment with the Creator's purpose.

The prevalent belief is that God created human beings. However, the truth is God became human. The human being is God's highest expression. Faith in this truth is the ultimate form of faith – the faith of God. Faith here means doubtlessly believing in your divinity; you have full conviction that you are one with God. When you utter something with this conviction, it has to come true. What is true for God is true for you.

The faith of God is the faith that God expressed in creating the world. God created the vast world in the faith that His highest creation would be a medium to experience Himself and express His divine qualities and boundless possibilities. God has taken the human form to experience His grandeur and sing praises of His glory. It is through the human form alone that God forgets His pristine nature and then rejoices in re-remembering it.

So, how do we realize and express the faith of God?

Having the faith of God means understanding that what is true for God is true for you, too. Here, God is the life essence, which is formless, beyond religion, beyond all beliefs. It is the Source of love, happiness, peace, and creativity. It is the living principle that permeates everyone and everything. It is eternal and nameless, yet each of us is blessed with a free will to call it in a way that helps us to arouse our faith.

What does the sea envision in the waves? What does God envision for human life? The expression of divine qualities and magnificent possibilities! But how does the wave see itself? The wave feels limited by its apparent boundaries and believes, "I am so little... I am insignificant... I have less than others."

Most people place their faith in their limiting beliefs rather than the faith of God, as evidenced in their daily conversations. When people scorn others or curse their own fate, they operate from their beliefs based on ignorance. By entertaining self-defeating thoughts and speaking negative words, people create only poison in their own lives and of those around them. They lower their consciousness, attracting toxic relationships, struggle, and scarcity.

When we say, "I cannot do this... My life is destined to be an endless struggle... No one loves me... I cannot trust anyone...," how do we regard ourselves? We consider ourselves helpless victims, lonely, poor, betrayed, deficient, or ill. But is this how God regards us? Not at all!

This is what God wishes to communicate through you. The voice of God speaks when you connect to the Source within. It reminds you of the truth of your grandeur: "You are an integral part of me... you are me! You have the same powers that I have."

Most people rarely heed this divine voice that whispers from within. When you say, "I am happy," God affirms, "You are Happiness." "I am happy" or "I am sad" emerge from mental conditioning and vary by situation, but happiness is our divine changeless essence. When you say, "I am a lover" or "No one loves me," God says, "You are love." When you say, "I am courageous," God asserts, "You are courage." If you say, "I am not creative," God declares, "You are creativity!"

Source-writing – the divine affirmations of God's faith

"I am an integral part of God... I am one with the divine essence... What is true for God is true for me." Do such words emerge within you? When you lend your voice to the faith of God, you create nectar in your life, attracting the very best according to your divine plan. Words that resonate with the faith of God serve as divine medicine, bringing health, prosperity, love, harmony, creativity, and fulfillment to your life.

A father wishes his child to write something. For the father to lovingly hold his child's hand and guide him to write, the child should be fully absorbed in the father's presence and available to the writing process instead of being distracted by myriad thoughts and external attractions. When the child is fully aligned with the flow of how the father guides his hand, what will the father write through him? That is akin to God writing through you! That is Source-writing.

Amid the constant flow of egoic thoughts in your everyday life, divine thoughts also emerge. You should be alert to identify and quick to verbalize them. You should give voice to divine thoughts. Let divine words flow in your voice and be written through your pen. What gets written by this voice are divine affirmations that are the declaration of truth originating from God.

Writing divine affirmations helps you align with your divine essence. Write them down as though God is addressing you directly, reminding you of your divine truth. These are not simply affirmations but divine expressions spoken from the standpoint of the Creator, helping you return to your true nature.

If you feel unhappy, ask yourself what God would say about unhappiness. He would say, "I have made you in My image to experience and express pure bliss. I am the Source of happiness." To express faith, feel this; speak it out mentally or loudly; write it down. As soon as you express this faith, you will shift your vibration to happiness.

Similarly, if you feel unloved, lend your voice to the divine affirmation, "I have made you in My image to experience and express pure love. This world is an expression of unconditional love. I am the Source of love." Speak this aloud, allow love to permeate your heart, and write it down. Love and forgive yourself unconditionally.

If you feel restless, irritated, or angry, write down the divine affirmation: "I have made you in My image to experience and radiate supreme peace. I am the Source of peace."

When the body is ailing, proclaim what God has to say about this body: "I have created you and this body in My image. It is whole and perfect. Let this body serve the expression of supreme consciousness."

Speak out these divine affirmations aloud and write them down several times so they enter and intermingle with every cell of your body. Like you interweave wool threads to make a sweater, interweave these divine affirmations with every cell of your body. By expressing divine affirmations, you elevate your consciousness and invite divine guidance into every aspect of your life. You begin to align with the divine plan, transforming challenges into opportunities for growth.

Using divine affirmations in daily life

To incorporate divine affirmations into your daily life, begin by quieting your mind and connecting with your inner self:

Connect with the Source: Before verbalizing a divine affirmation, enter a state of calm and visualize the Creator speaking directly to you.

Craft your divine affirmation: Draw from sacred teachings or intuitive guidance. For example, based on the Bhagavad Gita, you might write: "I act with devotion, trusting that God guides my steps."

Speak it aloud: Verbalize your divine affirmation daily. Feel the divine energy flowing through your words as you express faith in the Creator's plan.

Trust and surrender: After writing and verbalizing the divine affirmation, let go of your attachment to the outcome. Trust that you are aligned with the divine will and that everything will unfold at the perfect time.

By verbalizing these divine affirmations, you transcend ego-driven concerns and embrace the larger purpose of the Creator's plan. Whether inspired by the Bhagavad Gita, Buddhist, Jain, or Islamic teachings, divine affirmations help you resonate with the divine truth within.

The practice of writing from the Source

When you sit for Source-writing, it is a kind of writing meditation. Remain absorbed in the experience of the silence beyond thoughts, and the Source begins to write through your body-mind. In other words, you become a pen for the Source.

Don't fixate on what to write. Sit with pen and paper, not knowing what will be written. Wait to see what will emerge through the pen. Whatever emerges will be scribed without judgment, whether it makes logical sense or not.

So for writing from the Source, first connect with the Source, which requires silencing the mind's chatter. You can achieve this by using a writing technique called brain-dumping.

Our mind has two distinct functional aspects—the contrast mind and the intuitive mind. The contrast mind divides everything into two— good and bad, pleasure and pain, black and white, wrong and right, heavy and light. You must transcend this duality. The intuitive mind functions naturally to do anything in the best way without a personal agenda.

Cultivate the habit of sitting down daily and writing whatever springs to the mind, regardless of how random or insignificant the thoughts may appear. This form of writing may seem disorderly, repetitive, or even purposeless.

The contrast mind may judge what you write and stop you at certain places. However, you must allow yourself to freely write everything that comes to your mind without concern for quality or the insistence on flawless or sophisticated writing. Remember that you are doing it for your own sake, writing for your eyes only. This is called brain-dumping, which helps declutter the mind. This daily practice helps you tune into your intuitive mind, allowing you to become a medium for the voice of faith.

Whatever gets written during brain-dumping might seem negative, fragmented, or even silly, but it helps clear out all the worries, complaints, and distractions that clutter the mind. Writing down your thoughts about everyday stress at work or in relationships helps clear the way for creative inspiration.

Brain-dumping is essential for connecting with the Source and accessing the creative spark, especially for those who feel blocked. Many of us suffer from constant self-criticism. This negative inner voice relentlessly undermines confidence with doubts and negative remarks disguised as truth. Brain-dumping helps silence this inner critic and allows divine affirmations to flow more freely.

No matter your mood or the negative thoughts from your inner critic, you must write regularly. The common misconception is that writing can happen only when you are in a good mood, but that is far from the truth. Even when everything feels miserable, writing can happen from the Source. You must stop self-judgment and keep writing regardless of how stressed or distracted you may feel.

Brain-dumping helps you overcome inner barriers like fear, negativity, and self-doubt, leading you beyond self-criticism. The contrast mind is structured and linear and categorizes everything based on what is already known. It dismisses anything unfamiliar or creative as wrong or unsafe. By writing freely, you dissolve these reservations and fixations of the contrast mind and connect with the Source.

When the contrast mind is silenced, what emerges from the heart is free and creative. While the contrast mind insists on order and correctness, the voice of faith is open to being vulnerable and delights in the beauty and wonder of the unknown. Brain-dumping helps to quiet the contrast mind that doubts and judges your intuition. Writing without doubts or judgment paves the way for divine affirmations to flow unhindered.

As you continue writing, you reach a stage where you become empty from within. Then, writing from the Source begins. Usually, when you write, you think and then write. But when writing from the Source happens, thinking and writing happen simultaneously. You don't know what you are about to write; you learn about it only when it gets written. When you read what you have written, further thoughts stream from the Source, and you write more. This process goes on. This is how the ancient scriptures were written.

When you write as an individual, you write about your roles and the part you play in the drama on the world stage. But when you transcend the conditioning of the mind and the play of the ego, writing from the Source happens through you; you write for the Source.

What gets written this way brings health, prosperity, and love to your relationships and blossoms your creativity. The Source wishes to experience itself, open up, blossom, and express divine qualities like love, bliss, peace, patience, forgiveness, empathy, devotion, creativity, courage, and contentment through you. This is God's will. When it is fulfilled through you, the purpose of human life is fulfilled.

In this book, we have explored various writing techniques. There are many other paths to attaining the sublime state of God-realization, like listening to truth discourses, practicing meditation, and performing sadhana. These other paths can also help us easily connect to the Source.

Let your life be a reflection of divine inspiration. Write divine affirmations daily, and witness how they transform your relationship with yourself, the world, and the Creator. This alignment is the path to true fulfillment, peace, and joy.

Here are some divine affirmations that you can start with. Practice writing any or all of them down in your journal while reciting or singing them with melody.

I am one with the Divine Essence.

I am an integral part of God.

What is true for God is true for me.

I am love, I am happiness, I am peace.

I am perfect health, I am the reservoir of divine energy.

I am established in the realization of my true self.

I live in the experience of who I truly am.

I am free, I am freedom.

I flow smoothly as life unfolds. The divine will is my wish.

The ultimate purpose of my life is fulfilled.

I am in complete alignment with the highest expression of life.

I am the epitome of patience and courage.

Forgiveness is my nature.

I am trust, I am trustworthy.

The future always brings the best because today is the very best.

Thank You… Thank You… Thank You!

You may even take any of them and write it 21 times before starting your day.

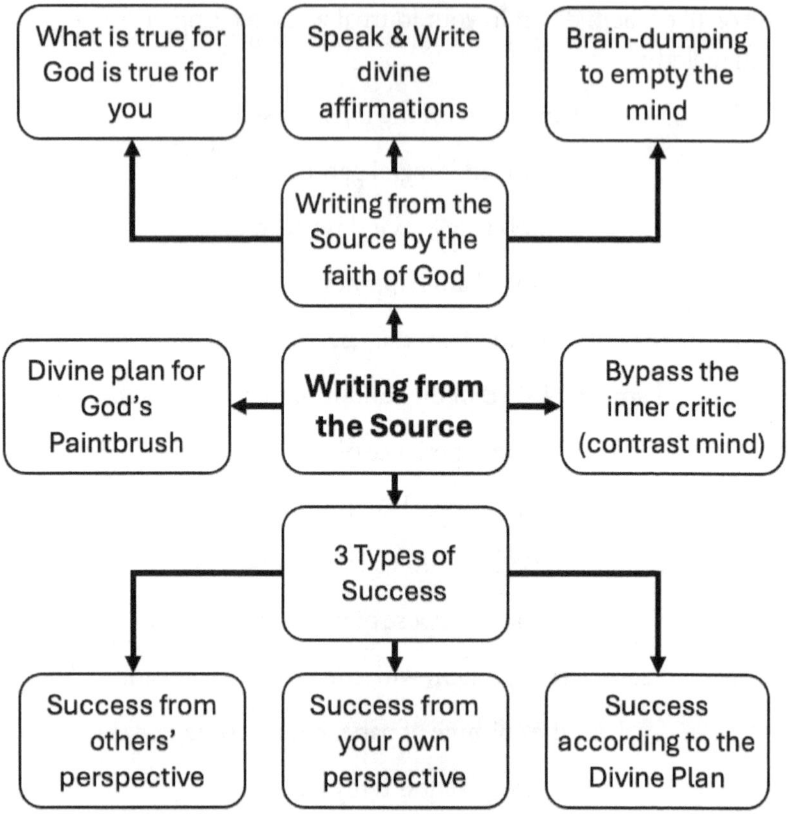

```
                ┌──────────────┐   ┌──────────────┐   ┌──────────────┐
                │ What is true │   │ Speak & Write│   │ Brain-dumping│
                │ for God is   │   │   divine     │   │ to empty the │
                │ true for you │   │ affirmations │   │     mind     │
                └──────▲───────┘   └──────▲───────┘   └──────▲───────┘
                       │                  │                  │
                       │        ┌─────────┴─────────┐        │
                       └────────┤ Writing from the  ├────────┘
                                │ Source by the     │
                                │   faith of God    │
                                └─────────▲─────────┘
                                          │
  ┌──────────────┐               ┌────────┴────────┐               ┌──────────────┐
  │ Divine plan  │               │                 │               │ Bypass the   │
  │ for God's    ├──────────────▶│ **Writing from**│──────────────▶│ inner critic │
  │ Paintbrush   │               │  **the Source** │               │(contrast mind)│
  └──────────────┘               └────────┬────────┘               └──────────────┘
                                          │
                                 ┌────────┴────────┐
                                 │   3 Types of    │
                                 │    Success      │
                                 └────────┬────────┘
                          ┌───────────────┼───────────────┐
                          ▼               ▼               ▼
                  ┌──────────────┐ ┌──────────────┐ ┌──────────────┐
                  │ Success from │ │ Success from │ │   Success    │
                  │   others'    │ │  your own    │ │according to  │
                  │ perspective  │ │ perspective  │ │the Divine Plan│
                  └──────────────┘ └──────────────┘ └──────────────┘
```

[11] - To know more, read the book *Awaken the Power of Faith* by Sirshree.

Scan this QR code to order your copy.

❖ ❖ ❖

You can mail your opinion or feedback on this book to:
books.feedback@tejgyan.org

About Sirshree

Sirshree's spiritual quest, which began during his childhood, led him on a journey through various schools of philosophy and meditation practices. He studied a wide range of literature on mind science and spirituality. After a long period of deep contemplation on the truth of life, his quest culminated in attaining the ultimate truth.

Sirshree espouses, "All spiritual paths that lead to the truth begin differently but culminate at the same point – Understanding. This understanding is complete in itself. Listening to this understanding is enough to attain the Truth." Over the last two decades, he has dedicated his life to raise mass consciousness.

Sirshree has delivered more than 4000 discourses that throw light on this understanding. He has designed a system for wisdom, which makes it accessible to all. This system has inspired people from all walks of life to progress on their journey of the Truth. Thousands of seekers join in a virtual prayer for World Peace and Global Healing daily at 9:09 am and 9:09 pm.

About Tej Gyan Foundation

Tej Gyan Foundation is a non-profit organization founded on the teachings of Sirshree. The Foundation disseminates Tejgyan – the wisdom that guides one from self-development to Self-realization, leading towards Self-stabilization.

The Foundation's system for imparting wisdom has been assessed by international quality auditors and accredited with the ISO 9001:2015 certification. This wisdom has been presented in a simple, systematic, and practically applicable form that makes it accessible to people from all walks of life, regardless of religion, caste, social strata, country, or belief system.

The Foundation has centers in more than 400 cities and towns across India and other countries. The mission of Tej Gyan Foundation is to create a highly evolved society by leading seekers from negative thoughts to positive thoughts and further, from positive thoughts to Happy thoughts. A 'Happy thought' is the auspicious thought of being free from all thoughts, leading to the state of supreme bliss beyond thoughts.

If you seek such wisdom that leads you beyond mere knowledge, dissolves all problems, frees you from all limiting beliefs, reveals the true nature of divinity, and establishes you in the ultimate truth, then it is time to discover Tejgyan; it is time to rise above the mundane knowledge of words and experience Tejgyan!

The MahaAasmani Magic of Awakening Retreat

Self-development to Self-realization towards Self-stabilization

Do you wish to experience unconditional happiness that is not dependent on any reason? Happiness that is permanent and only increases with time? Do you wish to experience love, peace, self-belief, harmony in relationships, prosperity, and true contentment? Do you wish to progress in all facets of your life, viz. physical, mental, social, financial, and spiritual?

If you seek answers to these questions and are thirsty for the ultimate truth, then you are welcome to participate in the MahaAasmani Magic of Awakening retreat organized by Tej Gyan Foundation. This is the Foundation's flagship retreat based on the teachings of Sirshree.

The purpose of this retreat

The purpose of this retreat is that every human being should:

- Discover the answer to "Who am I" and "Why am I?" through direct experience and be established in ultimate bliss.

- Learn the art of living in the present, free from the burden of the past and the anxiety of the future.

- Acquire practical tools to help quieten the chattering mind and dissolve problems.

- Discover missing links in the practices of Meditation (*Dhyana*), Action (*Karma*), Wisdom (*Gyana*), and Devotion (*Bhakti*).

About Books by Sirshree

Sirshree's published work includes more than 150 book titles, some of which have been translated into more than 10 languages. His literature provides a profound reading on various topics of practical living and unravels the missing links in karma, wisdom, devotion, meditation, and consciousness.

His books have been published by leading publishing houses like Penguin, Hay House, Bloomsbury, Wisdom Tree, Jaico, etc. "The Source" book series, authored by Sirshree, has sold over 10 million copies. Various luminaries and celebrities like His Holiness the Dalai Lama, publishers Mr. Reid Tracy, Ms. Tami Simon and Yoga Master Dr. B. K. S. Iyengar have released Sirshree's books and lauded his work.

The Source
Attain Both, Inner Peace and Worldly success

Awaken the Power of Faith
Discover the 7 Principles of the Highest Power of the Universe

To order books authored by Sirshree, login to:
www.gethappythoughts.org
For further details, call: +91 9011013210

SELECT BOOKS AUTHORED BY SIRSHREE

  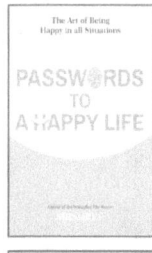 

   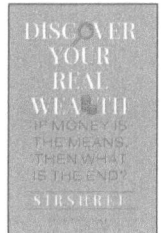

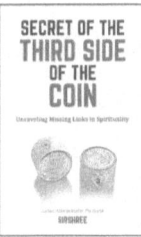   

To order these and other books authored by Sirshree
Visit **www.gethappythoughts.org**

Tej Gyan Foundation – Contact details

Registered Office:
Happy Thoughts Building, Vikrant Complex, Near Tapovan Mandir, Pimpri, Pune 411017, INDIA. Contact: +91 20-27411240, +91 20-27412576

MaNaN Ashram:
Survey No. 43, Sanas Nagar, Nandoshi Gaon, Kirkatwadi Phata, Off Sinhagad Road, Taluka Haveli, Pune district - 411024, INDIA. Contact: +91 992100 8060.

WORLD PEACE PRAYER

Divine Light of Love, Bliss, and Peace is Showering;
The Golden Light of Higher Consciousness is Rising;
All negativity on Earth is Dissolving;
Everyone is in Peace and Blissfully Shining;
O God, Gratitude for Everything!

Members of Tej Gyan Foundation have been offering this impersonal mass prayer for many years. Those who are happy can offer this prayer. Those feeling low or suffering from illness can receive healing with this prayer.

If you are feeling troubled or sick, please sit to receive the healing effect of this prayer. Visualize that the divine white healing light is being showered on earth through the prayers of thousands and is also reaching you, bringing you peace and good health. You can dwell in this feeling for some time and then offer your gratitude to those offering the prayer.

A Humble Appeal

More than a million peace lovers pray for World Peace and Global Healing every morning and evening at 9:09. Also, a prayer (in Hindi) to elevate consciousness is webcast every day on YouTube at 3:30 pm and 9:00 pm IST. Please participate in this noble endeavor.

www.ingramcontent.com/pod-product-compliance
Lightning Source LLC
LaVergne TN
LVHW041839070526
838199LV00045BA/1357